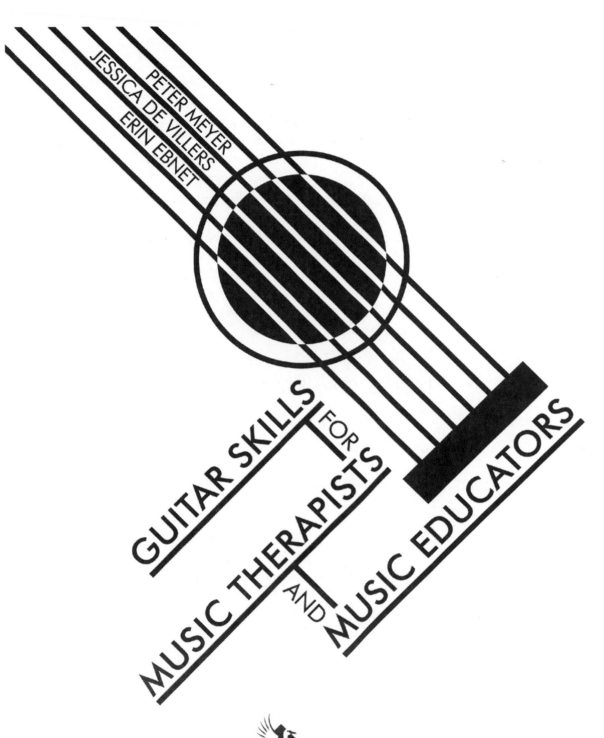

PETER MEYER
JESSICA DE VILLERS
ERIN EBNET

GUITAR SKILLS FOR MUSIC THERAPISTS AND MUSIC EDUCATORS

Barcelona PUBLISHERS

Guitar Skills for Music Therapists
and Music Educators

Copyright © 2010 by Barcelona Publishers

ISBN 13: 978-1-891278-56-3

2 4 6 8 9 7 5 3 1

Distributed throughout the world by:
Barcelona Publishers
4 White Brook Road
Gilsum NH 03448
Tel: 603-357-0236 Fax: 603-357-2073
Website: www.barcelonapublishers.com
SAN 298-6299

Cover design:
© 2010 Frank McShane

About the Authors

Peter Meyer received a B.M. in music therapy from the University of Minnesota in 2004. He received his NMT training in 2004. Peter graduated with an MA in music therapy from St. Mary-of-the-Woods College in 2008. He has presented at the American Music Therapy Association's (AMTA) Great Lakes and Midwestern Regional conferences on rhythm guitar and jug bands respectively. He has also presented on music therapy at the Huntington's Disease Society of America's national conference. Peter has been a professional guitar player over fifteen years. During this time he has taught private and group lessons. He was a teacher's assistant for the *History of Jazz* and the *History of African-American Music* from 2000-2004 at the University of MN. He has studied guitar with W.C. Handy Award Winners Paul Rishell, Ronnie Earl and John Cephas. In addition, he has shared the stage with James Cotton, Roomful of Blues, Ronnie Earl, and W.C. Clark.

Peter would like to thank Catherine Luiken for her love and devotion, Genevieve Grace for reminding him how great 3:00 A.M. can be, and Janet Meyer for teaching him about dedication. Peter would also like to thank his two co-authors, Jessica DeVillers and Erin Ebnet for their vision and dedication in making this possible. He would like to thank Elizabeth Giffin for all the helpful suggestions and blues musicians Paul Rishell and Annie Raines for being his self prescribed music therapy. Lastly, Peter would like to thank his students and the music therapists who have attended his workshops, for it was their input that helped to design the book.

Jessica De Villers received her Bachelors Degree in Music Therapy from the University of Wisconsin-Eau Claire in 2007. She studied French horn and Piano as primary instruments in her undergraduate coursework. She completed her Internship at the University Good Samaritan Specialty Center in Minneapolis, Minnesota. Recently Jessica started work towards a Master of Arts in Music Therapy at Saint-Mary-of-the-Woods College. In fall of 2007, Jessica completed the Neurologic Music Therapy (NMT) certification, and in the summer of 2008 she began working on the Hospice and Palliative Care Music Therapy (HPMT) credential. Currently Jessica resides in Eagan, Minnesota. She is currently employed as a music therapist at Woodbury Health Care Center, a long-term care facility.

I would like to dedicate this book to my family. Thank you for all the support you have given me with my passion for music and in my career as a music therapist. I would like to express my appreciation and dedication to Erin Ebnet and Peter Meyer for being wonderful friends and colleagues and making this all possible! Erin, thanks for your amazing knowledge of how to operate technology and Pete, thanks for your extensive guitar skills that inspired this book. I would also like to dedicate this book to my Danish and Cobblestone friends, who have taught me to live life to the fullest, make every moment count, and to make time for things you love, even when you have a million things to do! And to Todd, thanks for always being there to support the decisions I make in my career as a music therapist.

Erin Ebnet graduated from the University of Wisconsin-Eau Claire with a Bachelors Degree in Music Therapy, while studying voice as her main instrument. She has performed in various vocal and blues/rock ensembles and has presented at regional and national music therapy conferences on guitar. She currently lives in Iowa City, IA where she works for West Music providing contract music therapy services.

Erin would like to thank her co-author, Peter Meyer, for sharing his extensive knowledge of guitar skills which has helped her to become a better guitar player, musician and music therapist. She would also like to thank her co-author, Jessica De Villers, for her hard work, organizational skills and dedication to help make this book a reality. Finally, she would like to thank her family, friends and fellow colleagues who have encouraged and supported her over the years as she has pursued her career in music therapy.

Note to the Reader

Welcome to our book. This book is not intended for the complete music beginner, (although the beginner would undoubtedly benefit from the material); nor is this book intended to be a complete guitar manual. Rather, this book is designed to give the beginning player suggestions and pointers to improve their knowledge base and technique, thereby helping the novice player advance to an intermediate/advanced level with little effort. While many styles of playing will be included, all styles will not be introduced. Readers are encouraged to seek out additional resources. We have included several songs in the exercise sections of this book to provide more enjoyable practice experiences. While working your way through the book, we also encourage you, the reader to incorporate your own favorite songs into the various technique building exercises.

The DVD that accompanies this book provides demonstrations of each exercise listed in the book. So if you have questions about how to implement or practice any of the exercises, be sure to consult the DVD. The exercises in the book and the DVD are numbered the same.

We hope you enjoy the book and the DVD, and that you have fun learning how to play the guitar.

Peter, Jessica and Erin

Table of Contents

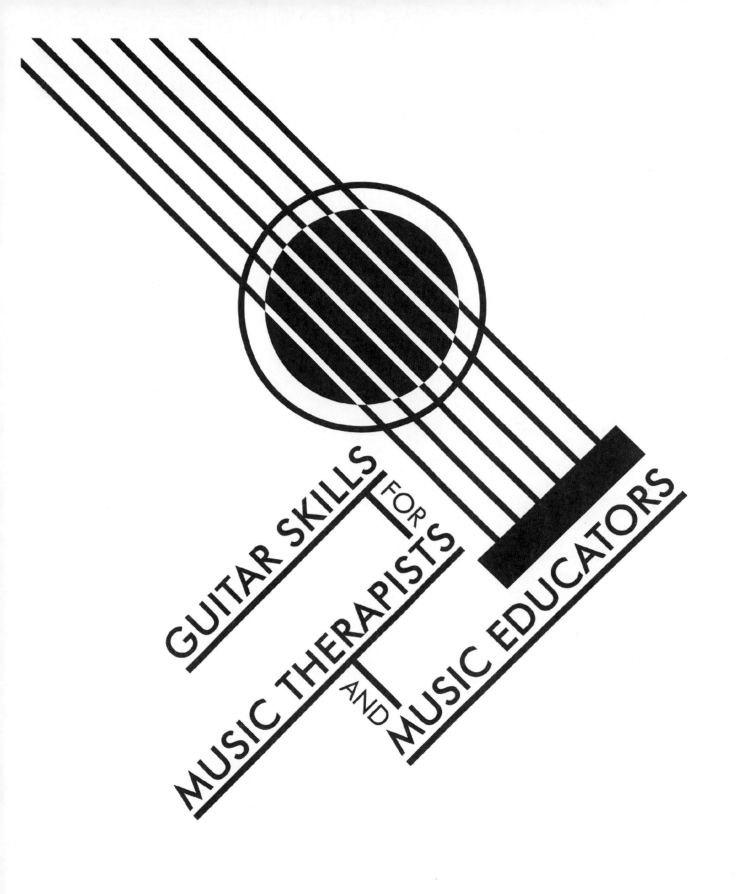

GUITAR SKILLS FOR MUSIC THERAPISTS AND MUSIC EDUCATORS

Introduction

Parts of the Guitar

Neck   Nut   Head

Saddle   Bridge   Body

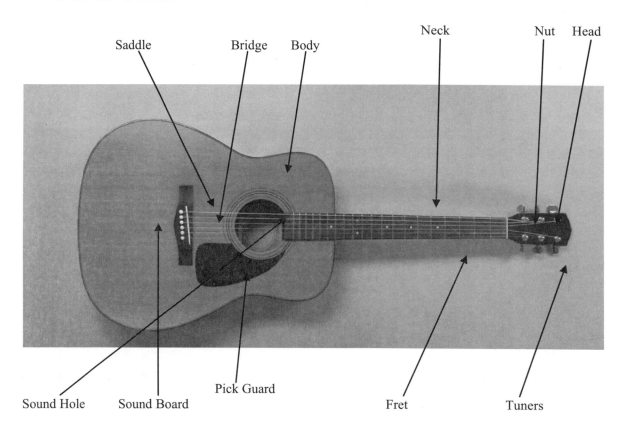

Pick Guard

Sound Hole   Sound Board   Fret   Tuners

Holding the Guitar

Now that you know the parts of the guitar, it is time to talk about holding the instrument. To hold the guitar while sitting, rest the middle bout of the guitar squarely on your knee, (whichever knee is more comfortable). Lean the guitar back into your chest and rest your strumming arm over the top. You should be able to move your left arm completely, and your right arm from the elbow down without having the guitar move. If the guitar moves, adjust your position until it does not. See DVD for photograph.

Holding the guitar while standing is quite similar to holding the guitar while sitting down. To stand however, you will need to adjust your guitar strap for the correct fit. To adjust the strap, hold the guitar while you are sitting down and adjust the length of the strap so that the guitar maintains the same position when you stand. This way you will not have to adjust your arms and the muscle memory you obtained while sitting will not be compromised. See DVD for photograph.

Introduction to Guitar and Music Concepts

Left Hand

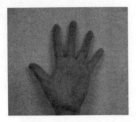

Thumb- T
Index- 1
Middle- 2
Ring- 3
Pinky- 4

Right Hand

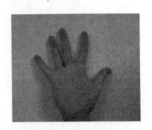

Thumb- P (pulgar)
Index- I (indice)
Middle- M (media)
Ring- A (anular)
Pinky- x, c, e

For your left hand, number your fingers starting with your index finger 1, 2, 3, 4. This can be especially tricky for piano players.

The right hand fingers are easy to remember. "P" identifies the thumb as the primary finger. "I" is for index. "M" is for *middle*. You can either remember that "A" is for anular or you will just have to remember that "A" does not have an English equivalent. The lettering for the pinky varies from text to text. This text will not identify a letter for the pinky, as we will not be incorporating it in any of the exercises in the book.

Notes

The notes in the western music alphabet are A, B, C, D, E, F and G. The smallest distance between two notes in the music system is a half step (or one fret on the guitar). Most of the notes have a whole step (two frets) between them. However, the exceptions are E and F and B and C. The rest have sharps or flats between them. A sharp (#) raises a note by one half step (one fret) and a flat (b) lowers a note by one half step (one fret). If this is unclear, see the notes on the neck of the guitar diagram on the next page.

Notes on the Neck of the Guitar:

Frets 1-12 (sequence repeats beginning on fret 13).

	Frets of the guitar going up chromatically											
E String	F	F#/Gb	G	G#/Ab	A	A#/Bb	B	C	C#/Db	D	D#/Eb	E
B String	C	C#/Db	D	D#/Eb	E	F	F#/Gb	G	G#/Ab	A	A#/Bb	B
G String	G#/Ab	A	A#/Bb	B	C	C#/Db	D	D#/Eb	E	F	F#/Gb	G
D String	D#/Eb	E	F	F#/Gb	G	G#/Ab	A	A#/Bb	B	C	C#/Db	D
A String	A#/Bb	B	C	C#/Db	D	D#/Eb	E	F	F#/Bb	G	G#/Ab	A
E String	F	F#/Gb	G	G#/Ab	A	A#/Bb	B	C	C#/Db	D	D#/Eb	E

String Names

The strings are numbered 1 through 6 and lettered E, B, G, D, A and E, high to low. An easy way to remember the strings is the acronym:

Every Boy Goes Downtown After Eating.

$$\begin{array}{cccccc} \textbf{E} & \textbf{A} & \textbf{D} & \textbf{G} & \textbf{B} & \textbf{E} \\ \textbf{6} & \textbf{5} & \textbf{4} & \textbf{3} & \textbf{2} & \textbf{1} \end{array}$$

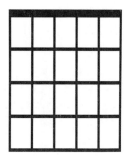

The Notes and Rests

Whole note- 4 beats

Whole rest- 4 beats

Half note- 2 beats

Half rest- 2 beats

Quarter note- 1 beat

Quarter rest- 1 beat

Eighth note- ½ beat

Eighth rest- ½ beat

Sixteenth note- ¼ beat

Sixteenth rest- ¼ beat

A dot (.) after any note increases it by half. For instance:

This note has three beats: A half note has two beats plus half of that would be three.

This note has a beat and a half: A quarter note has one beat plus half would be a beat and a half.

Standard Notation

This is an example of a staff. You will notice five lines and four spaces.

Lines from bottom to top = **E**very, **G**ood, **B**oy, **D**oes, **F**ine
Spaces from bottom to top = **F, A, C, E**

Time Signatures

The top number of the time signature refers to how many beats are contained in each measure. The lower number of the time signature refers to which note receives the beat.

The above time signature indicates that three beats are in a measure and that the quarter note gets the beat.

The above time signature indicates that six beats are in a measure and the eighth note gets the beat.

Counting

The illustration below demonstrates how the various beats would be counted:

1234   12 34   1 2 3 4 1&2& etc.   1e&ah 2e&ah etc

Key Signature

The key signature for a piece occurs at the beginning. You will notice in the first example that flats occur on the B line, the E space and the A line. That means all of those notes are flatted throughout the piece.

Tablature Notation

You may notice that tablature notation is different from standard notation in that there are six lines on the staff instead of five. The lines represent the strings. The 1st string is the line on top of the staff and the 6th string is line at the bottom. The numbers are the frets on which to place your fingers. The example above is an A minor pentatonic scale. It starts on the 5th fret of the 6th string. Notice that it does not indicate which finger to use. The next note is on the 8th fret of the 6th string. Next it moves to the 5th fret of the 5th string.

Major Scale

Major scales are constructed with a series of whole steps and half steps. Each major scale sequence is composed of: whole-whole-half-whole-whole-whole-half. This pattern will be the same regardless of where the scale is started..

C major

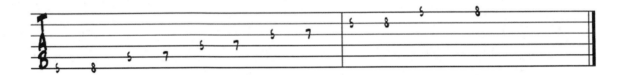

The Flat Scales

F major

Bb major

Eb major

Ab major

Db major

Gb major

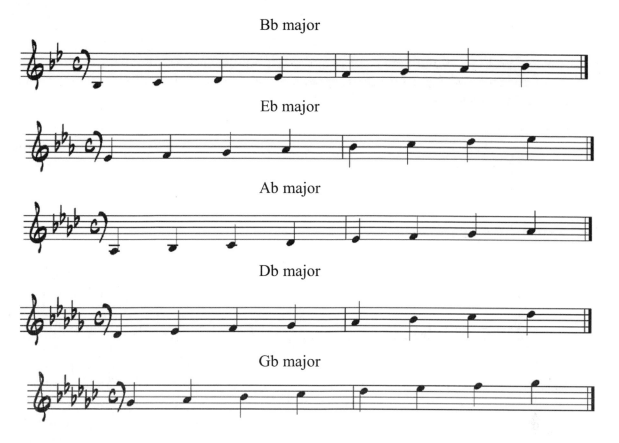

The Sharp Scales

G major

D major

A major

E major

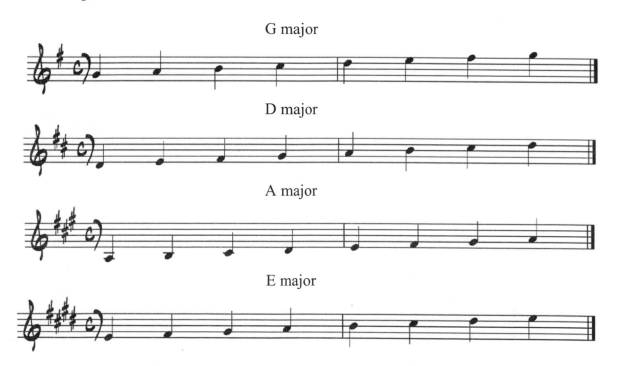

B major

F# major

Triad Chord Construction

Each note of the major scale is given a number. The first note is given a 1, the second is given a 2, the third note is given a 3, and so forth. Chords are constructed with the 1st, 3rd and 5th notes of the major scale. The chords with only three notes are called triads. Triads come in four varieties: Major, minor, diminished and augmented. You build a major chord with the 1, 3, and 5 of the major scale e.g., in the key of C the notes would be C, E, and G. You build a minor chord with the 1, flat 3 and 5 e.g, a C minor chord would be C, Eb and G. You construct a diminished chord with the 1, flat 3 and flat 5 of the major scale e.g., a C diminished chord would be C, Eb and Gb. Lastly an augmented chord would be constructed with the 1, 3 and sharp five of the major scale e.g., C augmented would be C, E, and G#.

Diatonic Harmony

The chords that fall in a given key are also given numbers. The I, ii, iii, IV, V, vi & vii o. The I, IV and V chords are the most common and they are the major chords. The ii, iii and vi are minor and the vii o is diminished.

8

Four Part Harmony

The seven is added after the triad in four part chords. In other words "7" chords are spelled with variations of the 1, 3, 5 and 7 notes of the major scale. You have two main types of major chords with a seven: a major 7 and a dominant 7. The major 7 is constructed with the 1, 3, 5 and 7 of the major scale and is called a "major 7" chord e.g., C major 7 contains C, E, G and B. A dominant seven has the 1, 3, 5 and flat 7 of the major scale and is simply called 7 e.g., C7 contains C, E, G and Bb. This can be confusing. A lot of people see the chord symbol for a C maj. 7 and play a C7.

You can also add a fourth part or 7 to the other triads as well. The beauty of this is that they also have similar names, the exception are the diminished chords. So for instance if you have a C minor triad you can add a 7 and it is called C min. (maj. 7). If you flat the seven it is called C min. 7. If you have a C augmented chord and add the major 7 you call it C aug. maj. 7 (C+ maj. 7). If you add the flat seven you call it C aug. 7 (C+7). The odd one of the bunch is the diminished triad if you add a major 7 to a C o triad you call it C tonic dim. If you add the flat 7 you call it C half-diminished, Cᴓ or C min.7 b5. If you double flat the seven you call it C diminished. This can also be confusing. How does one tell the difference between a C diminished triad or a C diminished 7 in a chord diagram? The answer is you don't. Assume it is the four part chord until your ears tell you differently.

9

Chord Diagram

The vertical lines in a guitar chord diagram represent the six strings (E, A, D, G, B, E or 6, 5, 4, 3, 2, 1) left to right. The horizontal lines in the diagram represent the frets. It should be assumed that the top line is the first fret unless another number appears beside the top line. A five (either Roman or Arabic numeral) appearing by the top line would indicate that the diagram begins on the fifth fret. The next line would be the sixth etc. Examine the diagram below of a D chord. Notice the 1st finger is on the 2nd fret of the 3rd string. The 2nd finger is on the 2nd fret of the 1st string. The 3rd finger is on the 3rd fret of the 2nd string. Notice the "x" by the 6th string. That indicates that the string should not be strummed. The "o"s indicate that the open string should be strummed.

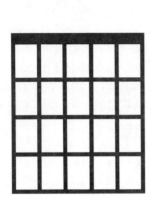 

Practicing

The easiest way to practice the techniques presented in this book are by applying them to your everyday work. Start by slipping a shuffle or a hammer-on into a basic folk song such as "You are my Sunshine" or "I've been Working on the Railroad" or other songs your clients/students request. Change the style. Try incorporating chuck or a different strumming pattern, exchange a basic chord for a barre chord. This practical approach will help learn the techniques very quickly just by starting with a simple change in how you play the songs that are already familiar to you.

Chapter I

The Basics

If you have never played guitar before, start with at the beginning of this chapter and go through it methodically. If you have some experience and are proficient in some keys but not all, simply go to the key you need practice, and apply the different strumming patterns at the end of this chapter.

Key of G

This book is designed to get progressively harder with each key. In my opinion the easiest key to play on the guitar is the key of G, followed by D, C, A and E. The key of G major and its relative minor E has one sharp, F#.

Key Signature

Open Position G Scale

When playing any note make sure you are on the tips of your fingers. Think about the tips being fence posts and the fret board being the ground. You want the fence posts to be straight, not slanted, otherwise all of your animals will get out. Also make sure your fingers are as close to the fret as possible without being on top of them, it is easier to push down.

One of the drawbacks to tablature notation is that it does not tell you which finger to use. To keep things simple, use the same finger as fret number. In other words, if a note is in the 3rd fret, play it with your 3rd finger. If a note is in the second fret, play it with your 2nd finger, etc.

All the notes in G in open position

The Chords: I, vi, IV and V7 chords

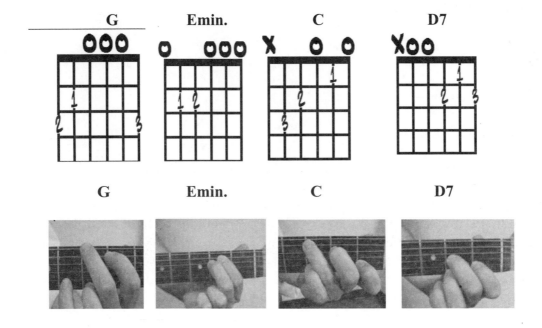

Chord Changing Exercises

See the next page for some exercises to help you switch between chords. We are first going to switch from G to Em. You want to identify fingers that stay in the same spot or keep the same shape. When switching between G and Em the 1st finger would stay the same. For these exercises, you will only be strumming down on the beat. This will help you develop a strong sense of time. Other strums will be incorporated later in the songs. Note: If you are getting bored with just strumming down, take a look at the other strums at the end of the chapter. Any of the strums can be incorporated into these exercises.

Ex. 1.01

Now let's switch between the Em and C. Notice that the second finger stays the same. Try the next exercise. Make sure you are keeping steady time.

Ex. 1.02

Next let's switch from C to D7. Notice the 1st finger stays the same.

Ex. 1.03

In the next exercise, we will be changing from D7 to G. This may be difficult in the beginning stages, but it can broken down slowly. Read the section "Advice on Changing Chords in Time" located after this exercise.

Ex. 1.04

Advice on Changing Chords in Time

If you are having difficulty switching chords try the following exercises. Timing is one of the most important things about playing guitar. More people (including your clients) are going to notice inconsistent rhythms before they notice incorrect chords. These exercises are designed not only to help with changing from one chord to another, but to develop timing skills as well. You can (and should) apply these exercises whenever you are having difficulty switching from one chord to another. Let's say, for instance, you are having difficulty moving between a D7 chord to a G chord. First, finger a D7. Before you strum the D7 chord visualize the G. Know where your fingers need to go. Think of any common fingers that might make this transition easier. Now begin the exercise. First strum a D7 for 4 beats using all down strokes. Now rest for 4 beats, using that extra time to try and get to G by beat 1. If you cannot comfortably make this switch in time, slow down the tempo. Conversely, once you are comfortable speed it up. When you can comfortably do this exercise at about 100 beats per minute, go on to exercise 1.06

Ex. 1.05

Ex. 1.06

For this exercise, use the same chords you were just practicing, but instead of 4 beats of rest, leave only 2. The same rules apply as they did in the previous exercise. If you cannot play it at the tempo you began with, slow it down until you can. Remember, if you are *practicing* it unevenly, you will *play* it unevenly.

Ex. 1.07

Now that you are more comfortable switching between the chords, strum for 3 beats and rest for 1 beat.

Ex. 1.08

This time try it without any rests. Once this is comfortable, you can incorporate the changes into a song. Remember these exercises are applicable to any chord changes.

In the last exercise you will be switching between all four chords.

Ex. 1.09

The Song

The chord progression and the songs will be introduced in this chapter. These chord progressions will reoccur throughout this book, however the lyrics and melody will not be recapitulated. It is assumed that you will be able to do this on your own.

For this song make sure you keep a steady strum, but unlike the exercises you want to strum down and up. Keep steady eighth notes. Count them 1 & 2 & 3 & 4 &. The arm should move down on the beat and up on the "and". This is the most important strum in the book! It is from this pattern from which the rest of the strums are taken.

Let's play this through a traditional '50's rock chord progression.

Ex. 1.10

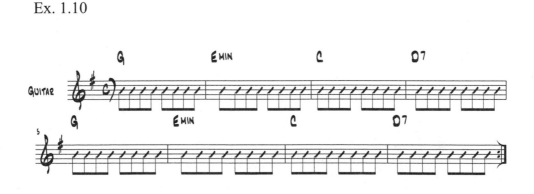

Note: Although all of the exercises in this chapter display only a quarter note rhythm, feel free to try any of the "Strum Patterns" located at the end of this chapter.

Key of D

Key Signature

The key of D and its relative minor of B have two sharps, F# and C#.

Open Position D Scale

All the notes in D in open position

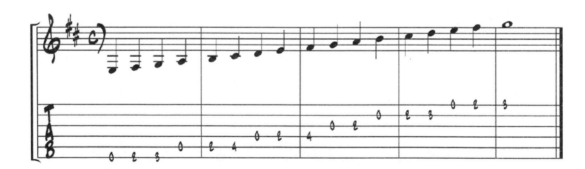

The Chords: I, vi, IV and V7 chords.

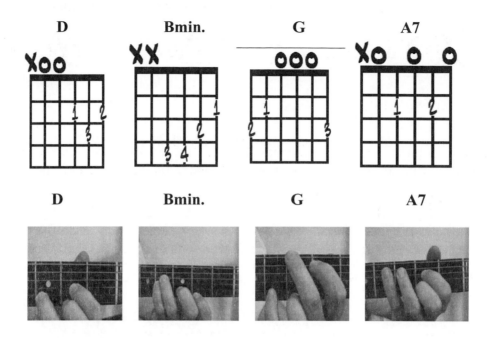

D   Bmin.   G   A7

Chord Changing Exercises

These exercises will follow the same format as the previous key. We will start with the I chord, D, going to vi chord, B minor. Begin with all down strokes. Once you are comfortable, try some of the other patterns in the book. If you are having trouble with this chord change, return to the "Advice on Changing Chords in Time" section

Ex. 1.11

Ex. 1.12: B minor to G

Ex. 1.13: G to A7

Ex. 1.14: A7 to D

This chord change is nice because the 1st and 2nd fingers keep the same shape. They just move physically up or down one string each, depending on the chord change.

Ex. 1.15: This will combine all of the chords in the key of D.

The Song

For this song, we are going to keep it simple and strum quarter notes on every beat. When you are strumming make sure all strums are moving down and be sure to accent beat one just a little bit. Count 1, 2, 3, 1, 2, 3.

Ex. 1.16: Down in the Valley

Key of C

Key Signature

C major and its relative A minor do not contain any sharps or flats.

Open Position C Scale

19

All the notes in C in open position

The Chords

For the "F" chord your 1st finger will lay flat and play two strings at this same time. This is especially difficult to do when the other fingers need to be on their fingertips. Begin by just playing the 1st finger. Make sure that both the first and second strings are making a sound. After that, add the 2nd finger. Make sure that you can hear the first three strings. If you cannot, adjust your fingers until you do. Then add your 3rd finger. Make sure all four strings are sounding. Remember, it takes time to gain the dexterity to lay one finger flat while the others are on the tips. Be sure you allow yourself time to develop this skill.

Here are the I, vi, IV and V7 chords.

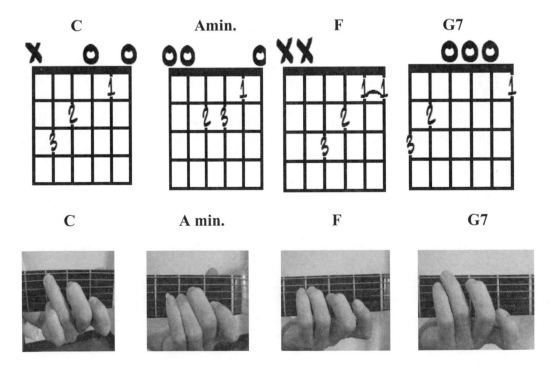

20

Ex. 1.17

For this exercise, we will begin with C and then go to A minor. Notice that the 1st and 2nd fingers remain the same.

Ex. 1.18

Moving between the A minor and F can be tricky. The first finger stays the same but now it lies flat. While keeping your 1st finger on the second string, roll your 1st finger down so now it is flat and covers the first string as well. This little motion will come in handy later on.

Ex. 1.19

In this exercise we will go from F to G7.

Ex. 1.20

In this exercise let's go from G7 to C

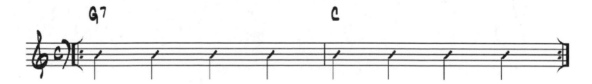

Ex. 1.21

Now we will combine all of the chords: C-Amin.-F-G7

The Song

This next song is a traditional English folk song, which was made popular by Simon and Garfunkel. It is not in the key of C major or A minor, but is in the key of D dorian. All three keys share the same key signature. The dorian mode and others will be discussed in greater detail in another chapter of this book. The i chord of D dorian is D minor. See the picture below for how the fingers look. As you play the song count 1, 2 &, 3 & and strum down, down-up, down-up.

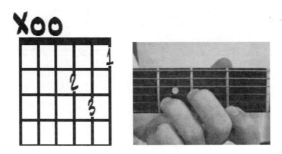

Ex. 1.22

Key of A

Key Signature

The keys of A major and F# minor have three sharps: F#, C# and G#.

Open Position A Scale

All the notes in A in open position

The Chords

Here are the I, vi, IV and V7 chords. For the F# minor chord play an E minor with your 3rd and 4th fingers on the fourth fret. Now take your 1st finger and point it out straight. Keeping the 1st finger straight simply lay it flat over the second fret so that it covers all six strings.

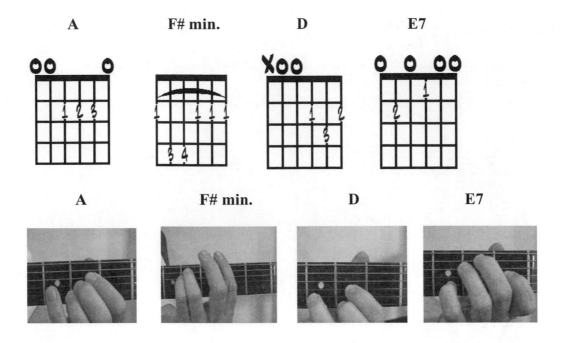

Ex. 1.23: A to F# minor.

This is a very difficult change. Be sure to practice it with rests, using the "Advice on Changing Chords in Time," before playing it straight through.

Ex. 1.24: F# minor to D.

While these chords do not have any common fingers it is much easier to switch from a barre chord to an open position chord.

Ex.1.25: D to E7

Keep your first finger down and just slide the finger from the second fret to the first fret on the third string.

Ex. 1.26: E7 to A

There are not any common fingers here, but if you have the others mastered, this switch should feel natural.

Ex. 1.27: All chords in the key of A.

This is a difficult progression. NOTE: The Advice on "Changing Chords in Time" can be used for multiple chords as well.

The Song

For this song count 1 2& 3 4&. Strum down, down up, down, down up.

This song is an African-American spiritual. Spirituals were collective compositions that often contained hidden meanings.

Ex. 1.28

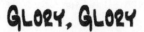

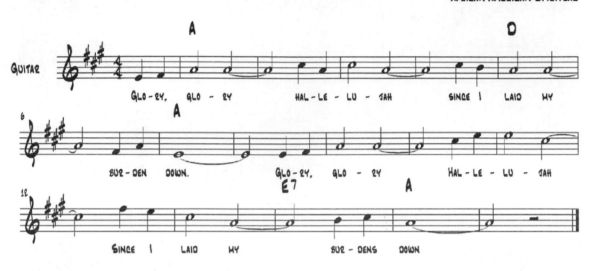

Key of E

The key of E has four sharps- F#, C#, G# and D#. It is also the last of the open position keys. The other seven keys are called closed position key because they will require barre chords for the majority, if not all of the chords.

Key Signature

Open Position E Scale

26

All the notes of E in open position

The Chords: I, vi, IV and V7

The C# minor chord is much like the F# minor chord but instead of playing an E minor with your 3rd and 4th fingers, play an A minor with your 2nd, 3rd and 4th fingers. Move that shape four frets higher, so that your 2nd finger is on the 5th fret. Point your first finger straight out, then lay it flat against the 4th fret. Also, note in the diagram the use of "4 fr." This indicates the fret at which the chord should be played. If it read "7 fr." the chord should be played at the seventh fret.

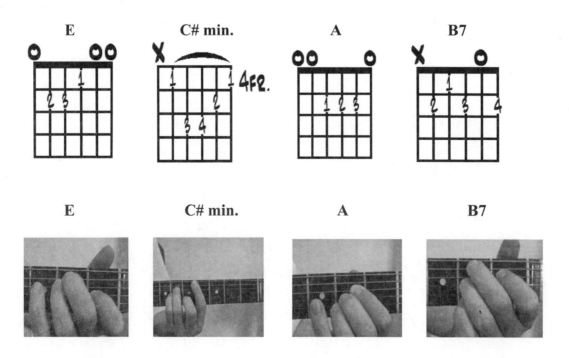

Ex. 1.29: E to C# min.

Again be patient with this chord change and practice it with the "Advice on Changing Chords in Time."

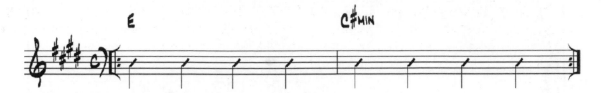

Ex. 1.30: C# min. to A

Ex. 1.31: A to B7

Ex. 1.32: B7 to E

Ex. 1.33: E-C# min.-A-B7-

The Song

For this song we will be using one of the most common strums in music therapy. While playing this pattern, you want to keep your arm moving down-up continuously but only hit the strings on 1, 2, the "&" of two, the "&" of three, four and the "&" of four. In other words, down down up up down up. While this strum is rhythmically interesting, many people become overly dependent on this pattern. Now that you have learned the music therapy strum, go forth and use it with discretion! Note: For ease of adding vocals, we will be playing two strum patterns per measure.

Ex. 1.34

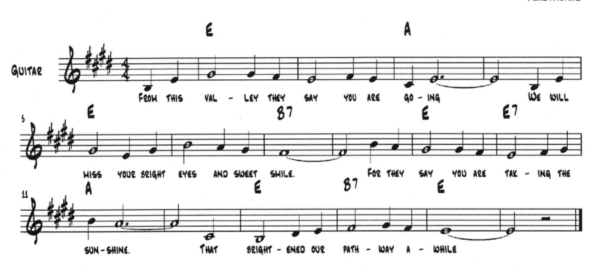

Last thoughts on strumming

The down-up strum is one of the most important strum for developing time. The patterns below are all extensions of the down-up strum. Simply "miss" the strings (a silent down or up) creates the difference in the pattern. Be sure to keep your arm moving in a perpetual motion even if it seems unnecessary.

D= Down strum
U= Up strum

If a letter is in parenthesis do not strike the strings. It is only there to remind you keep your arm moving. For ease of reading the () will be eliminated after Strum 4.

Ex. 1.35

Count	1	&	2	&	3	&	4	&
Strum 1	D	U	D	U	D	U	D	U
Strum 2	D	(U)	D	(U)	D	(U)	D	(U)
Strum 3	D	(U)	D	U	D	(U)	D	U
Strum 4	D	(U)	D	U	D	U	D	U
Strum 5	D		D	U		U	D	U
Strum 6	D			U				
Strum 7	D			U			D	
Strum 8		U	D		D			
Strum 9		U		U		U		U
Strum 10	D		D			U	D	U
Strum 11								
Strum 12								
Strum 13								

We have covered the first several strums in this chapter. Other strums are:

- Strum 7 is called the Charleston Rhythm. If you are strumming it slowly, it may be difficult to feel the groove. It may be helpful to start out slowly and increase the tempo as you become more comfortable with this strum.
- Strum 8 is a Rumba rhythm. If you combine it with strum 9, this creates a 3-2 clave rhythm that was popularized by early rock and roll artists like Bo Diddley.
- Strum 9 is a common Reggae/Ska rhythm.
- Strum 10 was popularized by the Indigo Girls.

The last three lines were left intentionally blank so that you could create your own patterns. Just be sure to strum down on the beat and up on the "&."

Recommended Listening

In order to achieve a solid groove, it is important to listen to artists who have strong and interesting rhythms. At this stage, we would recommend listening to the Indigo Girls, Melissa Etheridge, and James Taylor. These artists are able to create simple grooves that drive the song and support the melody.

Chapter II

I Know C, A, G, E and D…Now what?

By now through practice and applying what you have learned in the previous chapter, you should be comfortable to move on to some intermediate strumming techniques. These techniques will further your guitar playing, and enhance your sound and style. Once again, keep applying what you learn in this chapter to the songs you already know. This type of practice will help you learn the techniques faster.

Embellishments

Lifting or adding a finger can make your accompaniments more interesting. Take a look at the chords below. You will see the five open position chords. You will also notice some other markings. These refer to the chords becoming an add 9 chord, a 6 chord or a "sus" (suspended chord). Here they are in chord diagram form. They will be presented in the video using the tablature notation. You should also be aware that the embellishments for a major chord would be the same for a minor chord.

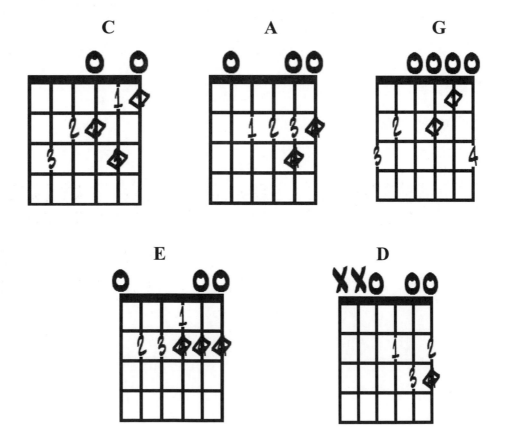

Ex. 2.01

Throughout this book, we will work progressively from easiest to most challenging. This is the E chord and some embellishments that can be added to it. Just finger an E and add your 4th finger to the third string to make it an E sus, add your 4th finger to the second string and it becomes E6. Add your 4th finger to the first string and it becomes E add 9. All of these can be used interchangeably. This exercise includes a familiar strum. If you want to really challenge yourself, make all the changes on the "&" of two. It may be difficult to change on an up strum, but it will add interest.

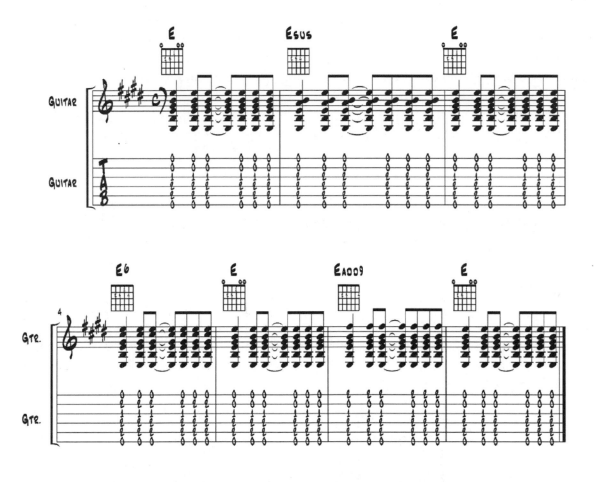

33

Ex. 2.02

These are the embellishments you can add to a D chord. Lift up your 3rd finger and the chord becomes D6. Lift up your second finger and the chord becomes D add 9. Put down your 4th finger on the third fret of the first string and it becomes D sus.

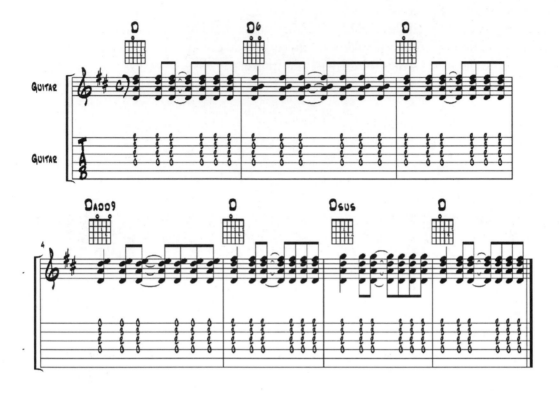

Ex. 2.03

When playing an A chord, lift up the finger that is on the second string, (typically the 3rd finger), creating an A add 9 chord. Adding the 4th finger to the third fret of the second string creates an A sus. chord. If you add your 4th finger to the second fret of the first string, it becomes A6.

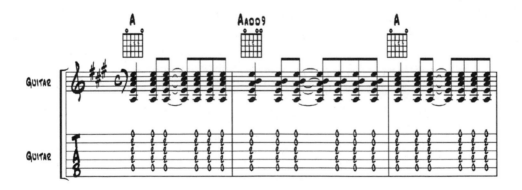

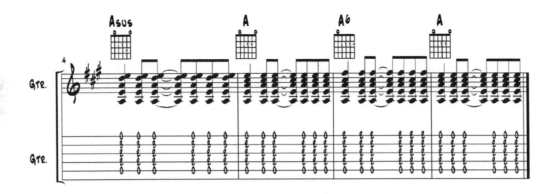

Ex. 2.04

Both the C and G chords can be difficult. We will start with C. C sus can be played two
different ways. You can add your 4th finger to the third fret of the string or you can use
your 1st finger to barre the first and second strings on the first fret. To make a C6, take
your 2nd finger and move from the fourth string to the third string. Be sure to get off your
finger tip with the 3rd finger so that it deadens the fourth string. The C add 9 can be
played by fingering a C chord and then adding your 4th finger to the third fret of the
second string.

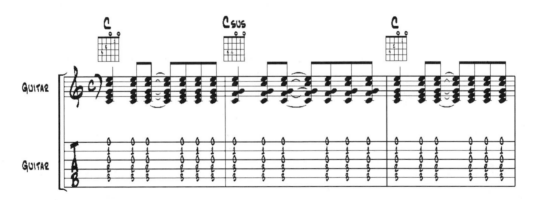

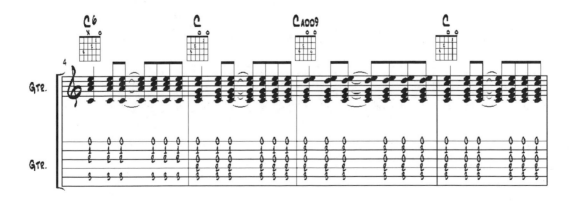

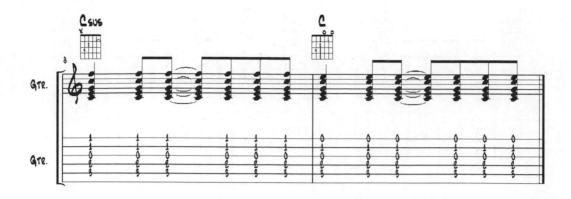

Ex. 2.05

In order to play the embellishments for a G chord, you must finger it with your 2nd, 3rd and 4th fingers. It may take some time to get used to if you normally finger it with your 1st, 2nd and 3rd fingers. Once this becomes comfortable, proceed with the exercises below. The G6 chord can be fingered two different ways. For the first method, take your 2nd finger and place it on the second fret of the fourth string. The other method is easier. Simply lift up your fourth finger leaving the first string open. To finger a G add 9 chord, add your 1st finger to the second fret of the third string. For the G sus. chord add your 1st finger to the first fret of the second string.

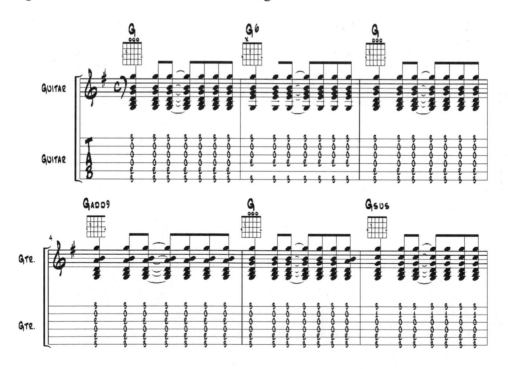

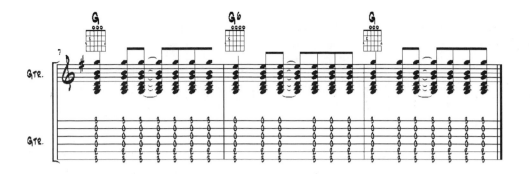

The Song

Now let's try the embellishments with a common '50's chord progression. Below is just one suggestion as to where to add ornamentation. Remember you can add any of the suspensions, 6's or 9's and to any song. Let your ear decide how little or how much you want to add.

Ex. 2.06

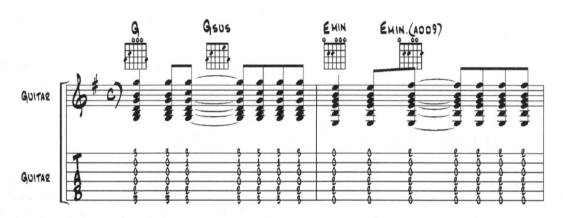

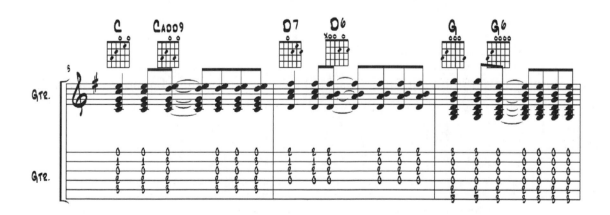

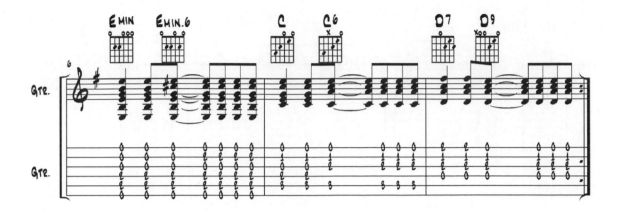

The Chuck

The chuck adds a percussive effect to one's guitar playing. Rather than pressing down and letting a chord sound, one lifts up the fingers, keeping them in contact with the strings. This produces a percussive a sound, which sounds like the word "chuck," (thus the name). Try getting the "chuck" without fingering any chord yet. Do this by laying your fingers gently over the six strings.

The easiest open position chords on which to achieve the "chuck" sound are D, E and A. For these chords, strum like you normally would, however, when you are adding the "chuck," aim for the adjacent strings your fingers are playing.

When to play the Chuck

While one can play the "chuck" anywhere rhythmically speaking, as we will discuss in a later chapter, first we will add it to the 2nd and 4th beat of a measure. Try strumming steady eighth notes. Now lift up on beats 2 and 4. Make sure you press back down on the "&'s" of both. It should sounds like a snare drum hit. Chucks are notated with an "X" over the note head.

Ex. 2.07

While playing a D, lift up your fingers on the 1st, 2nd and 3rd strings, but not too much. Be sure you do not hear anything but a percussive effect.

Ex. 2.08

While playing A, lift up the fingers on the 2nd, 3rd and 4th strings. Make sure you are only strumming those strings with the chuck.

Ex. 2.09

While playing E, lift up your fingers on the 3rd, 4th and 5th strings.

Ex. 2.10

The C and the G provide the greatest challenges for the "chuck." The problem is that you do not have a group of adjacent strings to aim for. To achieve the "chuck" with the C chord, roll your 3rd finger so that it dampens the strings. This is a little tricky if you are going to keep time. Practice this for awhile until it starts to feel comfortable. Note: This one might take a week or two to play correctly.

Ex. 2.11

When playing G, try using whatever finger is on the 5th string. Some people play a G with their 1st, 2nd and 3rd fingers. If this is the case use the 1st finger to achieve the "chuck." If you finger the G with your 2nd, 3rd and 4th fingers, roll your second finger to produce the "chuck."

Now let's try it in a song. This chord progression can be found in songs such as "You are my sunshine."

Ex. 2.12

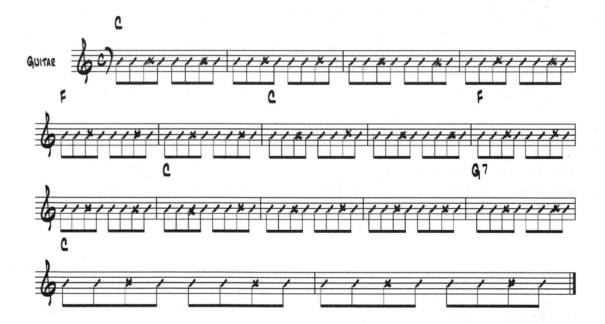

Palm Muting

This technique is hard to describe. Make sure you watch the DVD to see how and where your palm should be placed. What you want to do is take the heel of your hand and rest it on the saddle of the guitar. When you strum you should get a muted sound. If you are getting no sound, then you are pressing too hard. If the strings are ringing out, you are either not pressing hard enough or you are strumming strings that are not muted. When you palm mute you probably will not be able to cover all strings. So, much like the "chuck," just strum the strings that are muted. Once you have the mute mastered, try lifting it up on beats 2 and 4 to really drive the song. Be sure to watch the DVD while practicing these exercises.

The Song

Typically the palm mute is used to add variety to the sound of the guitar. If you are playing a repeating chord pattern such as in a blues or I, vi, IV, V progression, the sound may become boring. To enliven it, try adding the muted effect on the verse and lifting it up on the chorus.

The line above the exercise is to indicate when to use the palm mute. You will notice the first four measures employ the palm muting technique. Do not use the palm mute for measure 5 through 8.

Ex. 2.13

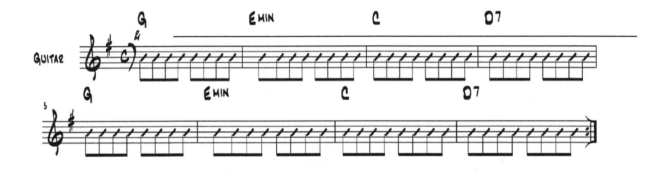

Staccato Playing

This method is often confused with the "chuck." Like the "chuck" it involves lifting up the fingers of the left hand to mute the strings. Unlike the "chuck" the lifting happens immediately after striking the strings. This technique is almost exclusively used with barre chords, however, it can be used with a chord that has a set of adjacent strings (e.g., A, D and E). Listen closely when you try this. Make sure you are not "chucking." As in the previous exercises, like the "chuck," be careful to play only the strings with your fingers on them, otherwise undesired notes will get notes ring out.

Ex. 2.14

Now let's try playing staccato with the chords from the African-American spiritual

Ex.2:15: Glory, Glory

Some thoughts on 2 and 4 and developing a strong sense of time

You may have noticed that we are placing a great deal of emphasis on the 2nd and 4th beat of the measure. The 2nd and 4th beat are referred to as the backbeat which is probably the most significant African-American contribution to music. There is a strong backbeat in most forms of contemporary music, from blues to jazz to country to rap. Accentuating the 2 and 4 really creates the groove. Try putting on some of your favorite music and clapping on 1 and 3. Something just doesn't feel right, does it? Now try clapping on 2 and 4. Not only does it feel correct, most likely you will want to move to the beat. This relates directly to clinical applications, especially ones in which we, as music therapists are facilitating movement.

Ex. 2.16

In order to develop timing skills, break out the metronome. Set the metronome to 100 bpm. Practice some down up strumming until you get comfortable. Now set the metronome to 50 bpm. The metronome is going to serve as your backbeat. Practice strumming so the click is now falling on beats 2 and 4. It can be hard to get the hang of it, but stick with it. With continued practice, your sense of time will improve.

Chapter III

Fingerpicking

Now that we have the basic chord shapes and strumming patterns down, we can move on to fingerpicking techniques. Using fingerpicking techniques in your playing will change the style and presence of the music. You may see different client responses by changing the style of your playing. For example, a music therapist using fingerpicking techniques while playing a song on guitar for a client expressing anxiety or pain, may be more likely to elicit a more relaxed response than when using strumming techniques. Arpeggio, alternate, and "Travis" picking styles are introduced as basic yet very complementary fingerpicking styles to further the development of your guitar skills.

Before we get started let's review the letter names for the first four fingers on the right hand:

P= Thumb
I= Index
M= Middle
A= Ring

Arpeggio Pick

The literal translation for arpeggio is "harp like." It has come to mean playing a chord one note at a time. For these exercises your index finger of your right hand will play the 3rd string, your middle finger will play the second, and your ring finger will play the first. Repeat this pattern across all chords. The thumb, one the other hand will move around the 4th, 5th and 6th strings depending on the chord. Try these exercises and keep in mind that all the hand patterns work for the minor chords as well.

Ex. 3.01

Ex. 3.02

Ex. 3.03

Ex. 3.04

Ex. 3.05

Once you are comfortable with doing P, I, M, and A, try varying the I, M and A. The examples below demonstrate only the C chord, but can be applied to other chords as well.

Ex. 3.06

Ex. 3.07

Ex. 3.08

Ex. 3.09

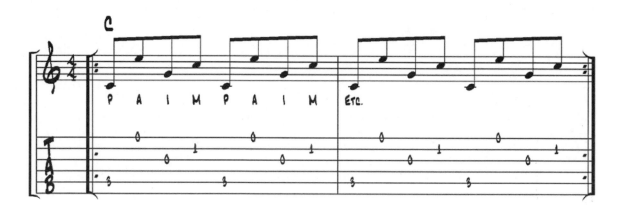

Ex. 3.10

Now let's try it with "Scarborough Fair." This will be a little different because you need to change chords in ¾ time. First, play the suggested pattern, then experiment by making up your own.

Scarborough Fair

Alternate Pick

This pattern is called the alternate pick because the thumb alternates with the fingers. Since you are already comfortable moving the thumb between stings with the arpeggio pick this one should not be a problem. If it is, review the arpeggio pick. Next, practice the examples and then apply them to the chord progression of Ex. 3.12.

Ex. 3.11 : Alternate Pick Exercises

Note: As with the arpeggio picks, you can switch your finger order as long as you continue alternating your thumb and fingers (e.g., P-M-P-I or P-I-P-A).

   Ex. 3.12

Next let's apply the same pick to the '50's rock and roll progression that was introduced in chapter 1.

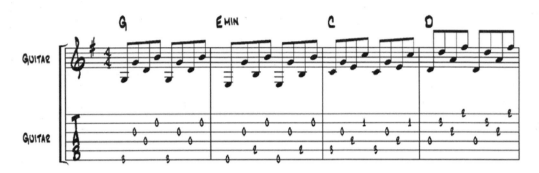

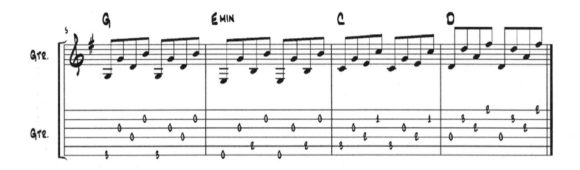

Travis Pick

The Travis pick is named after Merle Travis, the country-Western star. However, it was in existence long before Travis was playing it on hit records. The pattern was developed in the Piedmont region of the Carolinas. It came from the slaves that were imported from West Africa, who were the probable descendants of the Mande people. The Mande played an instrument called the Kora, which is played in a way that is similar to the Travis pick.

The primary characteristic of this pick is that the thumb keeps the beat. Below are a series of four exercises. The first consists of the thumb keeping time. The second adds the middle finger. The third adds the index, and the last is the official Travis pick. Keep in mind that any pattern with a steady thumb can be considered Travis picking (so the alternate pick is a version of the Travis pick). However, the "official" Travis pick is what is presented here.

Ex. 3.13

In this exercise the thumb keeps the beat. Be sure to begin this slowly. It will become more complex very shortly.

Ex. 3.14

Now your middle finger and thumb play together on beat 1 in a pinching sort of motion.

Ex. 3.15

Your index finger will play the third string on the "&" of beat 2.

Ex. 3.16

This is the "official" Travis pick. Just add the middle finger on the "&" of beat 3.

Ex. 3.17

As you play different chords, the only thing that changes is what string your thumb plays. Be sure to note how D differs from the rest. Here are the remaining open position chords.

Ex. 3.18: See next page for instructions.

In the above exercise, try the Travis pick through this familiar chord progression. Before you begin, try it with the full barre F.

F

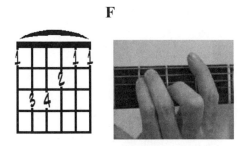

A couple more things

Now let's try the Travis Pick with a few embellishments. Does this sound familiar?

Ex. 3.19

You can also use the thumb to provide the accompaniment for a melody. An example of this can be found in the American folk song below. Listen to the example on the DVD. It is played straight. You can also add palm muting to the bass and emphasize beats 2 and 4 to really drive the song.

Ex. 3.20

SKIP TO MY LOU

TRADITIONAL-ARR. BY PETER MEYER

2009

Chapter IV

Flatpicking

Flatpicking is term used to describe the technique of by playing with a pick. Since it is not a fingerpick, it is called a flatpick. The technique typically involves playing bass notes.

The Bass-Brush or the Boom-Chuck

The next accompaniment style we will introduce can be called a bass-brush or a boom-chuck. We prefer to call it the former so as not to confuse it with the "chuck," which is a different technique entirely. The bass brush includes the alternating bass tones that you learned in fingerpicking, however, instead of using your fingers, you use a pick. Here are some examples to try with the five basic open position chord shapes. Remember that these can apply to the minor chords as well. Try playing these exercises as straight quarter notes or alternating quarter and eighth notes.

Ex. 4.01

Be sure to strum down on the beat and up on the "&."

Ex. 4.02

Ex. 4.03

Ex. 4.04

Ex. 4.05

The Song

Now let's apply these techniques while playing "Down in the Valley." Notice that you will have to make slight adjustments for time.

DOWN IN THE VALLEY

TRADITIONAL

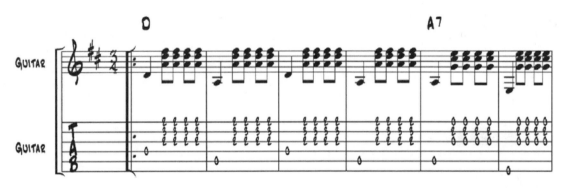

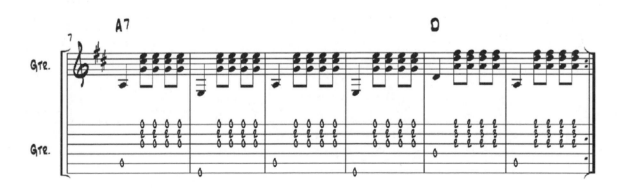

Hammer-ons

The next technique that will be used in called the "hammer" or the "hammer-on." The name is fairly self-descriptive, as you will see. Finger a C chord. Play the bass brush as you normally would, however, when you reach beat 3, lift up your 2nd finger and pluck the open 4th string. Now with all your finger strength and without plucking the string again, hammer (hit) your second finger onto the 4th string. If you didn't get any sound, your 3rd finger may not be on its tip. If that is not the case, you may not be getting enough force with the hammer-on. This is really a challenging technique. A lot of people tend to slow down before their finger comes in contact with the fingerboard. In order to correct this, try visualizing your 2nd finger going through the fingerboard and hitting the back of the neck. We have found through teaching experience that this little visualization goes a long way.

Ex. 4.06

Now let's try it with the other chords.

Ex. 4.07

Ex. 4.08

Ex. 4.09

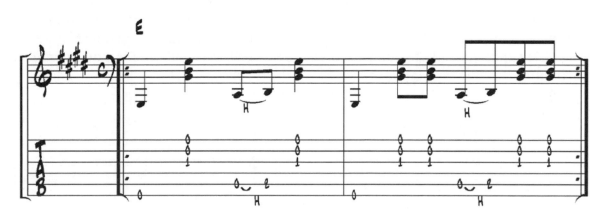

Ex. 4.10

The Song

Now try applying this technique to the song in the '50's rock chord progression.

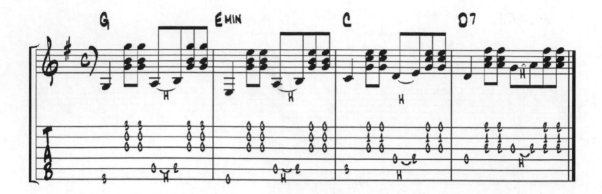

Bass Runs

Bass runs can be played either chromatically or diatonically. It is important that the notes lead to the next chord in the progression. For instance if the progression is a G chord to a C chord, the bass needs to move stepwise toward the C. This movement could be G-A-B to end on C, A-A#-B ending on C. Either choice indicates that C will be your next prominent note. Try the following examples in each key. Be sure to note that these are only some suggestions. Let your ear and your own creativity guide you in exploring other possibilities.

Ex. 4.11

Ex. 4.12

Ex. 4.13

Using the techniques in the key of A, try playing this riff that was made popular by Johnny Cash.

61

Ex. 4.14

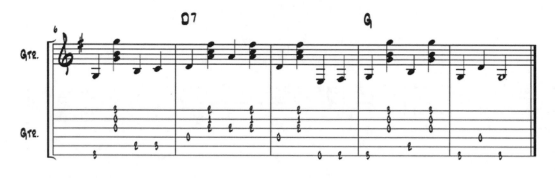

Ex. 4.15

Ex. 4.16

Bass Runs and Hammer-ons

This exercise is intended to help you to start thinking about how to combine all the presented information. It is okay to use hammers with the bass runs and any fingerpicking style. You can also incorporate the add 9s and the suspensions to your flatpicking. Here are some examples.

Ex. 4.17

Ex. 4.18

64

Ex. 4.19

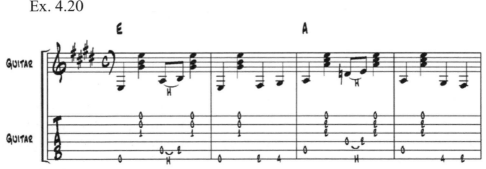

Ex. 4.20

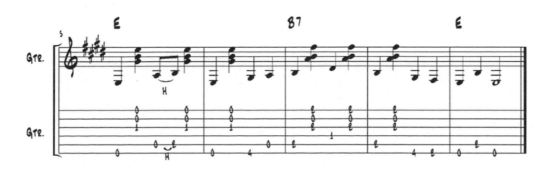

65

Ex. 4.21

The Song

For this next exercise we will again be using the song, "Glory, Glory." We will be incorporating both the bass runs and the hammer-ons. You may find that you can only play the bass runs at first. This is normal. With more practice, the hammer-ons will come.

GLORY, GLORY

African American Spiritual

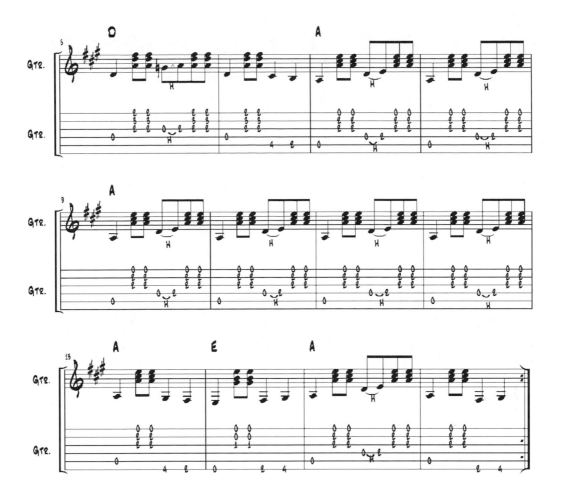

Flatpicking

So far we have been learning the basics of flatpicking. Often times when people refer to flatpicking guitar, they refer to a style that features the melody in the bass, which is what we will practice next. Let's try it with "Glory, Glory" again.

Ex. 4.22

GLORY, GLORY

AFRICAN AMERICAN SPIRITUAL

Chapter V

Barre Chords

The barre chords are the bane of many a guitar player. They are difficult to play and it takes a while to get them to sound good. Consequently, many people avoid them by playing only open chords, especially people who are already accomplished musicians on another instrument. However, the problem with avoiding them is that the sound of the chords will never improve. So, to the reader who is new to or has been avoiding barre chords, tell yourself now "It is OK to sound bad for a little while." Give yourself the time and patience you would give to your clients. If you practice the barre chords diligently for eight weeks, you are guaranteed to play them effectively.

Note: If you want a little more coordination practice without the finger pressure, skip this chapter and go to chapter 6. Once you are able to do the exercises in chapter 6 return to these chord shapes.

The E-Shape Barre Chord

Barre chords come in five main shapes, the C, A, G, E and D shapes. However, the two least difficult to play are the E and the A shapes. They get this name because the shape of the notes not being played resembles the E and A chords. Play an E chord as you know it, see Figure 1. Now play it in all its variations: minor, 7, minor 7. Really take a look at how these shapes appear. Now finger the E chord with your 2nd, 3rd and 4th fingers, and see Figure 2. Do the same thing, go through all the variations. Are you feeling comfortable with this? If so, you are ready to barre.

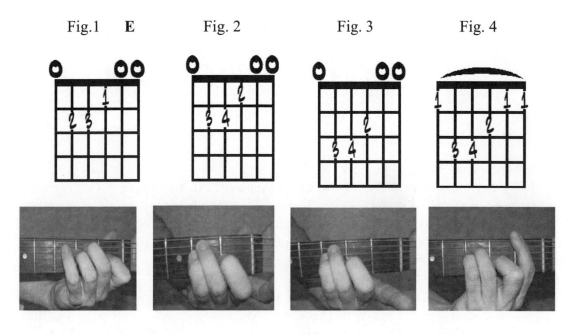

Fig.1   E   Fig. 2   Fig. 3   Fig. 4

Keep fingering the E chord with your 2ⁿᵈ, 3ʳᵈ and 4ᵗʰ fingers. Slide the chord up one fret, see Figure 3. Your 2ⁿᵈ finger should be in the second fret. Now take your index finger and point it straight outwards. Keeping it straight, bring your finger back so that it covers all six strings, see Figure 4. Push down and strum. How does it sound? If all the strings are sounding muffled, you need to increase the pressure. This is done only by *practice* and developing strength in your hand. Think about working out. How long does it take to see results? This is no different. If only one or two strings are not sounding, this may be because your hand is not in the correct position. Keep adjusting your fingers until it sounds accurate.

To determine what chord you have just played, try thinking of it like this: one fret=one ½ step, therefore a ½ step higher than E would be an F. Now thinking about the chord in relation to an E shape, you can create an F minor chord by lifting up your 2ⁿᵈ finger. This pattern holds true as you move it up the neck. If you were to form this chord on the 2ⁿᵈ fret you would be playing an F#. The next fret would be G followed by G# and so on. To familiarize yourself with the notes on the neck, play the chords through the circle of 4ths: C, F, (Bb, Eb, Ab, Db), Gb, (B, E, A, D), G. The notes in parentheses are there to help you remember the pattern, it spells BEAD, twice. Playing barre chords through the circle of fourths can be monotonous. So to get extra practice time in doing that, practice this pattern as you watch TV. Remember, this exercise is mainly for muscle memory, so you do not have to think about it too much.

Below is a fingerboard diagram to help you with the note location.

	Frets of the guitar going up chromatically											
E String	F	F#/Gb	G	G#/Ab	A	A#/Bb	B	C	C#/Db	D	D#/Eb	E
B String	C	C#/Db	D	D#/Eb	E	F	F#/Gb	G	G#/Ab	A	A#/Bb	B
G String	G#/Ab	A	A#/Bb	B	C	C#/Db	D	D#/Eb	E	F	F#/Gb	G
D String	D#/Eb	E	F	F#/Gb	G	G#/Ab	A	A#/Bb	B	C	C#/Db	D
A String	A#/Bb	B	C	C#/Db	D	D#/Eb	E	F	F#/Bb	G	G#/Ab	A
E String	F	F#/Gb	G	G#/Ab	A	A#/Bb	B	C	C#/Db	D	D#/Eb	E

E Shape Progression

This next chord progression will be a workout. So before you attempt this song try incorporating a barre chord into one of the songs you have already learned. For instance play, the A chord in the song "Glory, Glory" on the 5ᵗʰ fret, while playing all of the other chords in open position. In this song or a song of your choice, introduce additional barre chords one at a time, as you are able. This type of gradual incorporation of the barre chords will allow you to progress without feeling overwhelmed.

When you feel ready for multiple barre chords, try the exercise below. It is an Aeolian chord progression that can be heard in the song "All Along the Watchtower" by Bob Dylan or the solo section to "Stairway to Heaven" by Led Zeppelin. You have to keep the shape moving and your hand will get no rest. It will hurt but by the time you are able to sing the Dylan song from start to finish, you should have no fear of barre chords. Start with the C minor chord on the 8th fret, Bb on the 6th fret and Ab on the 4th fret.

Ex. 5.01

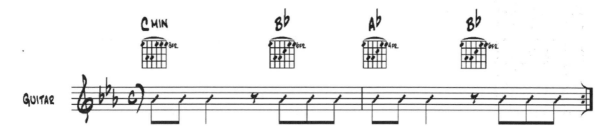

The A Shape Barre Chord

Now let's try another barre form. Start by fingering an A chord, then work through its variations: Amin., A7, and Amin.7. Now finger the A major chord with your 2nd, 3rd and 4th fingers. Finger all variations. Go back to A. Move the shape up one fret. Now take your index finger and point it straight outwards. While keeping your finger straight, lay it across the fret so that it covers all six strings. Push down and strum. If the chord doesn't sound, review the steps for effective barring techniques under the E shape section.

Fig. 1 **A**   Fig. 2   Fig. 3   Fig. 4

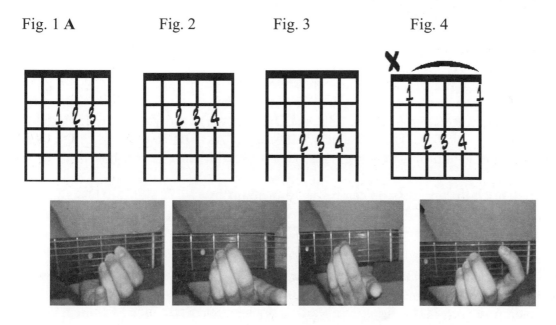

A Shape Alternate Fingering

Fig. 5

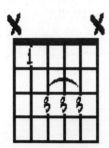

To become more familiar with this section of the neck, play the A shape chord through the circle of fourths. Remember that the fingerboard is chromatic. Therefore, barring the first fret with the A shape will result in an A#, the second fret will be B, the third C. Refer to the fingerboard diagram if you are having difficulty.

A Shape Progression

As stated earlier, playing the songs that consist solely of barre chords can cause a great deal of muscle fatigue as well as frustration. Try incorporating this barre chord shape into a song you already know. For example, play the D in "Down in the Valley" as an A shape barre chord on the 5th fret. The A7 can still be open. As with the previous exercise, gradually incorporate additional barre chords, then proceed to the exercise below.

This mixolydian chord progression can be heard in songs by J. J. Cale, Eric Clapton and Cream. It will start on the 7th fret for E, 5th fret for D. Be sure to maintain a pattern of strumming down on the beat and up on the "&."

Ex. 5.02

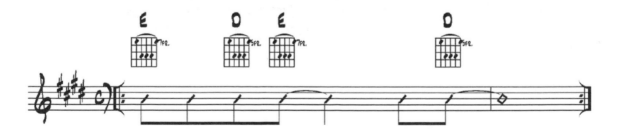

Combining the forms

Before playing the next song, try taking both the E shape and the A shape through the circle of fourths simultaneously by moving between the E and A shape on the same fret. For example, begin by playing C chord on the 8th fret (E shape) then move to F as an A shape (also 8th fret). Now continue to move through the circle of fourths in this manner.

Combination Progression

This chord progression is in the style of the Rolling Stones. The Em and the D should be A shape chords. All the rest should be E shape.

Ex. 5.03

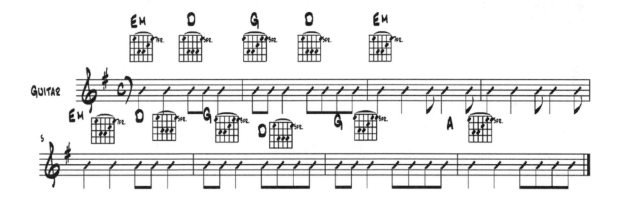

Conclusion

Although this is the shortest chapter, it most likely will prove to be the most work. It will take some time for your fingers to develop the positioning for the Barre shapes. Do not get discouraged, it will come in time. Practicing the circle of fourths should help you to develop the positioning of the chords for speed and accuracy.

More Barre Chords

As previously mentioned there are several other barre chord shape possibilities including the D, the G and the C shapes. After you are comfortable with the E and A shapes, try some of the other voicings. All are in root position unless noted with an empty circle. The circle indicates is where the root note is.

C Shape

C   Major   Minor   7   Maj. 7

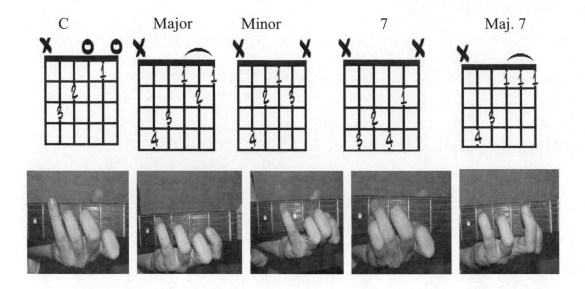

min. 7   min.7 b5   o

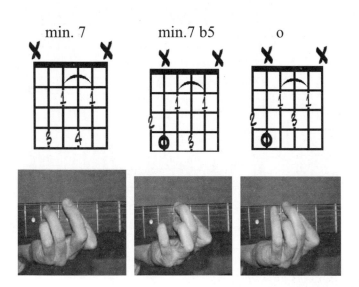

A Shape

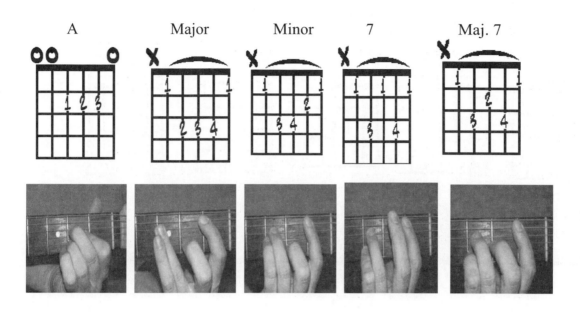

A   Major   Minor   7   Maj. 7

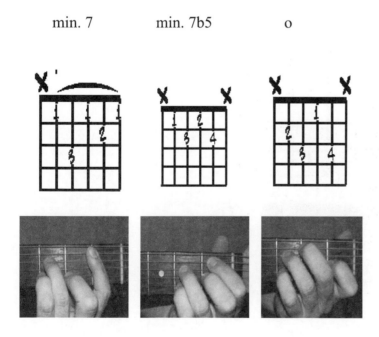

min. 7   min. 7b5   o

75

G Shape

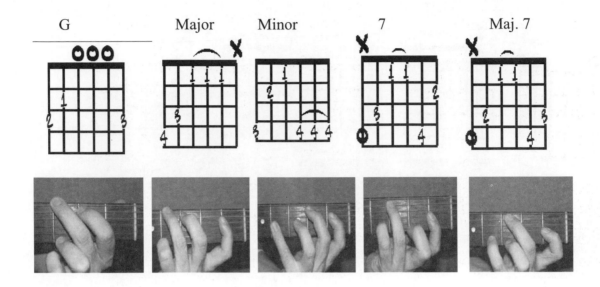

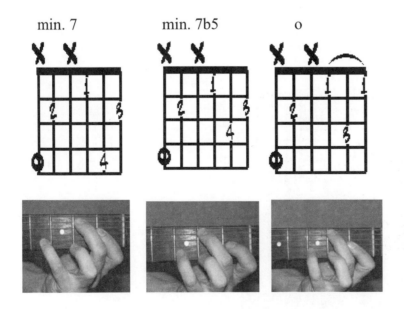

E Shape

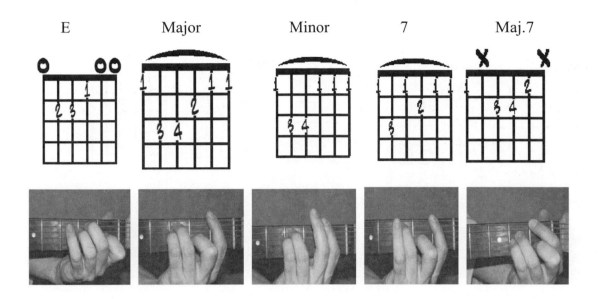

E	Major	Minor	7	Maj.7

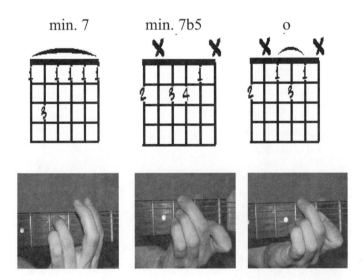

min. 7	min. 7b5	o

D Shape

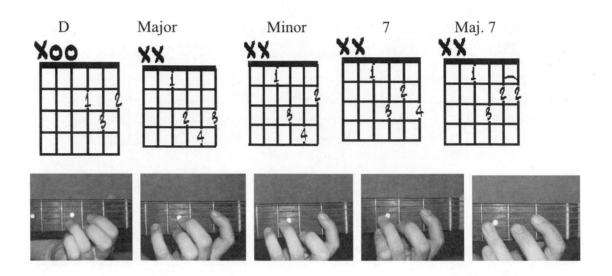

D · Major · Minor · 7 · Maj. 7

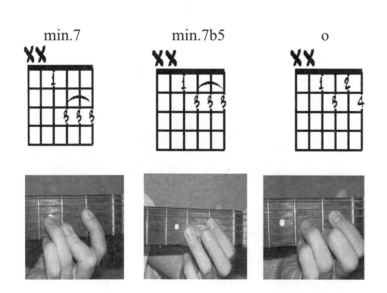

min.7 · min.7b5 · o

Chapter VI

Power Chords: Are you ready to rock?

 Power chords are the foundation of rock and roll. They figure prominently in a variety of different songs from the fifties to present day. The power chord was first heard in Eddie Cochran's "Summertime Blues."

What makes a chord a power chord is that does not contain a 3rd of the triad, it only contains the root and 5th. There are two main shapes for the power chord. The first one starts on the 6th string (Fig.1), and the second starts on the 5th string (Fig. 2). As with the barre chords, practice these chords through the circle of fourths.

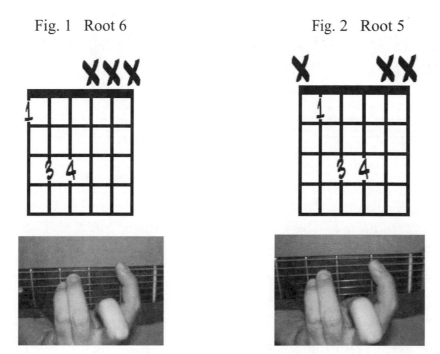

Let's start with the root 6 and learn a quintessential guitar riff. Note: All chords in this example are in the root 6 form.

Ex. 6.01

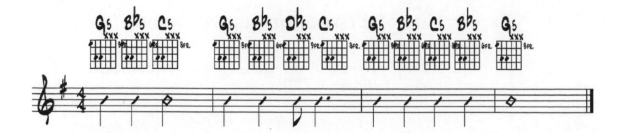

Here is a song that combines both chord shapes. The A5 is played on the sixth string the D5 and the E5 are played on the fifth string.

Ex. 6.02

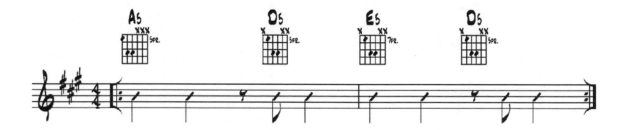

This last exercise can be heard in the Kinks' "You Really Got Me." It is very challenging. Once you have mastered these two bars, move the pattern around to different strings and frets. You will be able to hear the song.

Ex. 6.03

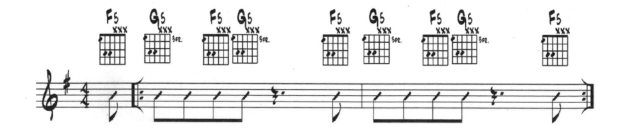

At this point, we have covered the basics of rock guitar power chording. Now increase your repertoire by branching out and playing your favorite rock hits.

Chapter VII

The Blues

The blues began as an African American art form around the late nineteenth century, although its roots can be traced back further. For a more in depth overview on the blues and its history, we would suggest reading Lawrence Cohn's book *Nothin' but the Blues*.

Musical Characteristics

The blues has several identifiable chord progressions: the 12-bar blues, two different 8-bar blues progressions and "Ice Cream" changes. We will begin with the twelve bar progression in the key of A. Notice you have a long time on the "I" chord. Be sure to remain on it all four measures. The chord progressions for this exercise are in the key of A.

The 12-Bar

Fig. 1

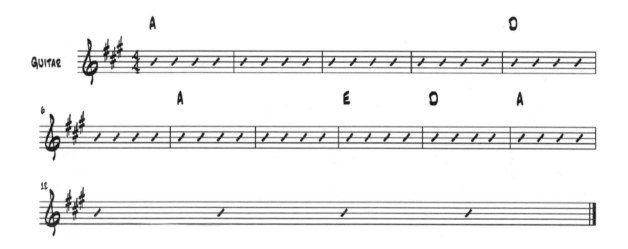

The 8-Bar

The blues has two 8-bar progressions. Let's learn the first one by following the chord progression for "Key to the Highway" or "Sittin' on Top of the World." This chord progression is in the key of G.

Fig. 2

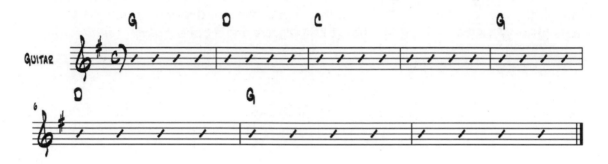

The Other 8-Bar

The other 8-bar blues chord progression can be found in songs like "Nightlife" or "It Hurts Me Too."

Fig. 3

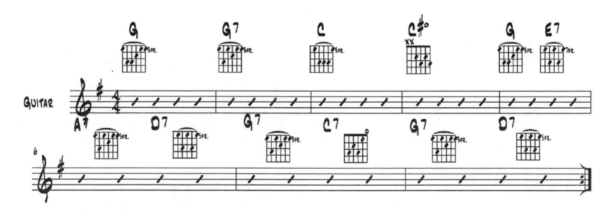

Note: If you can spice up any song by adding some "Gospel Chords." The first "Gospel Chord" is the #IV diminished chord. In gospel music, a good rule of thumb is to play a #IV diminished chord after the IV chord, as long as it is heading back to the I. Notice the IV to the #IV movement in the above exercise. Now try add the gospel progression to the song "You are my Sunshine." Add it on the tenth measure. Notice how it adds a "fresh" feel to a familiar tune.

Another chord that figures prominently in gospel music is the III7 chord. If the progression is moving from a I to a V, you can add the III7, fig. 4. Add it to the second measure of this song, (in this case a B7). Once you are comfortable go back and add it to "You are my Sunshine" in the eighth measure for a nice effect.

Fig. 4

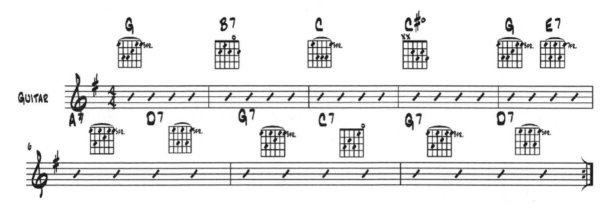

Ice Cream Changes

It is unknown where the term "Ice Cream Changes" originated. Many songs from the 1920's to 50's use this chord progression. Two recognizable songs that inclue Ice Cream Changes are "Walk Right In" by Gus Cannon and his Jug Stompers or "Alice's Restaurant" by Arlo Gutherie.

Fig. 5

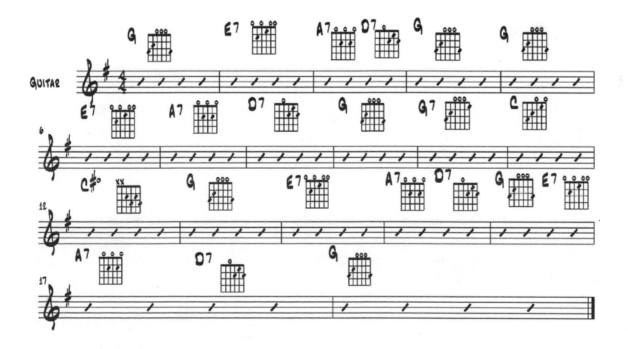

Blues Accompaniment

Give the repetition within the blues chord progressions, it is useful to add stylistic rhythms to keep the sound interesting. The first thing we will demonstrate is the shuffle. The first examples are the open position shuffles using C, A, G, E, D and F. The rest of the examples will be in movable form.

Ex. 7.01

To play a blues shuffle in C, finger the chord as you normally would. Then drop your second finger to the 3rd string. Be sure that your 3rd finger deadens the fourth string to prevent unwanted sounds. Make sure to swing the eighth note.

Ex. 7.02

Playing the shuffle in G is a lot like playing it in C. Finger G as you normally would, then take the finger that is on the fifth string and move it to the fourth string. Allow the finger that is on the sixth string to deaden the fifth string. Again, remember to swing the eighths.

Ex. 7.03

The E, A and D shuffles only require two strings. For E, put your 1st finger on the second fret of the fifth string. Play the open E string and the fifth string on beat one. On beat two, add your 3rd finger to the fourth fret of the fifth string. Continue in this fashion. To make it easier, keep your 1st finger down throughout.

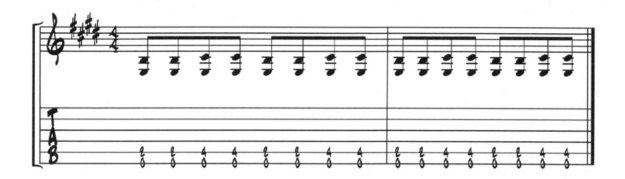

Ex. 7.04

To play the A shuffle, repeat the same shape that you played for the E shuffle, but move it physically down one string. Be careful to only strum the fifth and fourth strings.

Ex. 7.05

For the D shuffle, use the same pattern as for E and A, but move your fingers up to the third string.

Now try the shuffle with a 12-bar blues progression.

Ex. 7:06 Open 12-bar in A

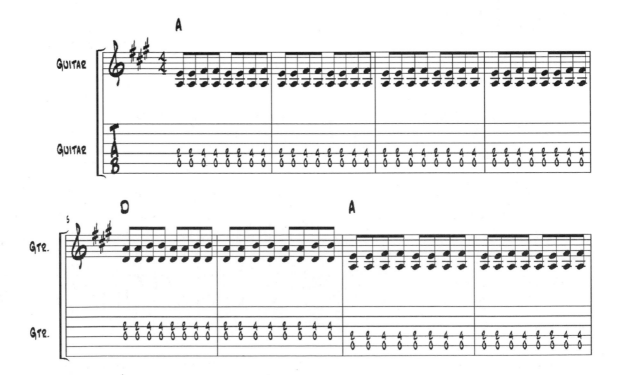

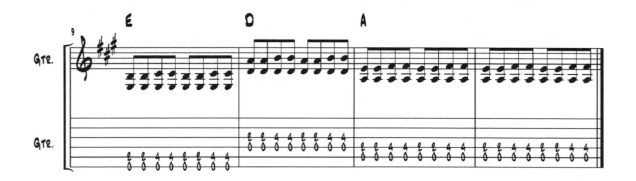

Ex. 7.07: Open 8-bar in G

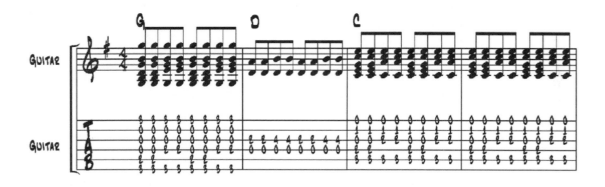

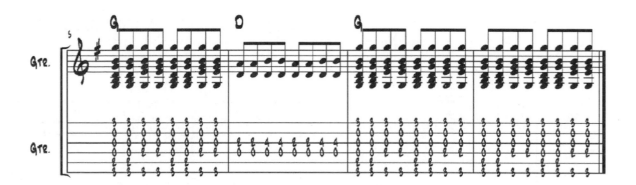

Moveable Shuffle- For the moveable shuffle, play a power chord without your pinky. Take your pinky and play the string that your 3rd finger is on two frets higher. If you can't make this stretch, try moving your hand to a higher fret so that it will be less difficult.

Ex. 7.08: Here is an example with the root note on the sixth string.

Ex. 7.09

Now let's try it with the root note on the fifth string. Again you can play these through the circle of fourths.

Ex. 7.10: 12-Bar with Moveable Shuffle Patterns in C.

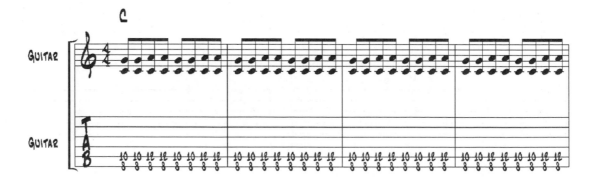

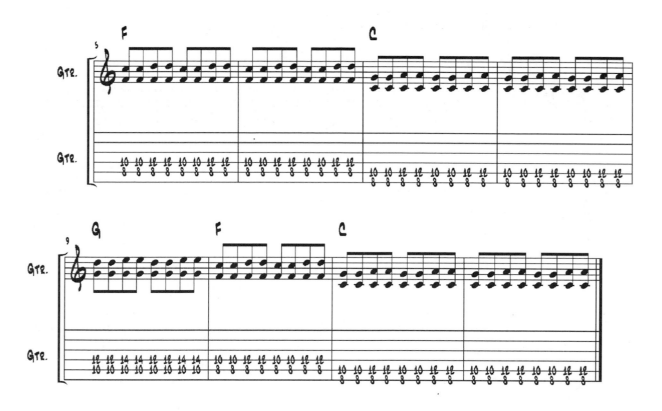

The boogie bass is the sound that you hear in the left hand of piano boogie woogie. We will first simulate this with the open chord shapes. Next we will progress to moveable shapes. These are less difficult than the shuffles.

Ex. 7.11: Open Boogie Bass in C.

For the next four exercises use the same frets as fingers.

Ex. 7.12: Open Boogie Bass in A

Ex. 7.13: Open Boogie in G

Ex. 7.14: Open Boogie in E

90

Ex. 7.15: Open Boogie in D

Moveable Boogie

The moveable boogie bass pattern is based around the shuffle shape. Begin the pattern
with your 1st finger, then 3rd then 1st, then 3rd and then fourth. Note: Each new string you
play in this pattern begins with the 1st finger.

Ex. 7.16: Moveable Boogie in A beginning on the 6th string.

Ex. 7.17: Moveable Boogie in D beginning on the 5th string.

Ex. 7.18:   12-bar with Open Boogie Bass

7.19: Moveable version

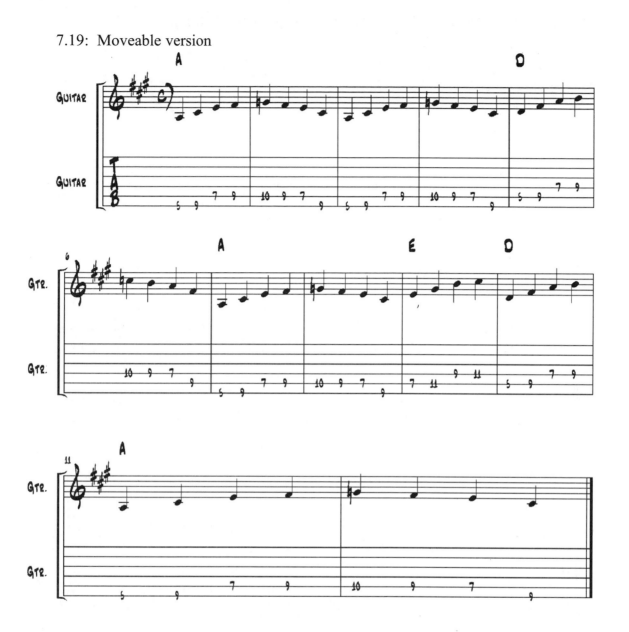

The Box-The box is named for its square shape. These are also moveable shapes. Try the first three examples then incorporate them into the 12-bar progression.

Ex. 7.20

Ex. 7.21: 12-Bar Box

As with all the moveable shapes (shuffles, boogie, box etc.) practice them through the circle of fourths.

Don't forget the Travis Pick

To get "Ice Cream" changes to sound stylistically correct, play them with the Travis Pick and open position chord. Make sure to accent 2 and 4.

Ex. 7.22

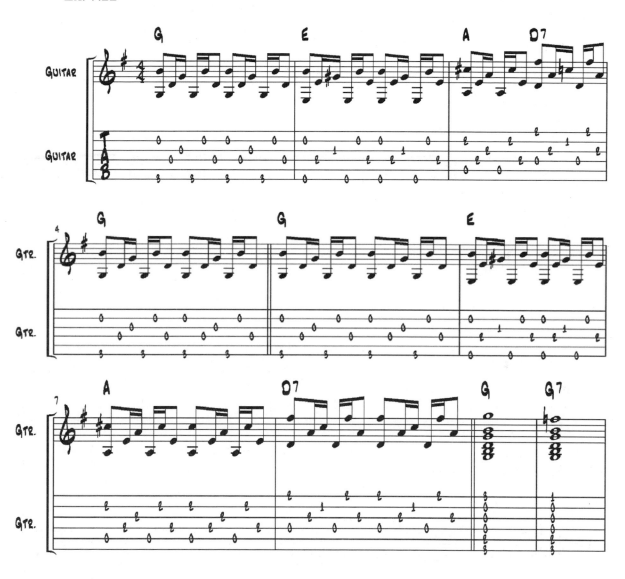

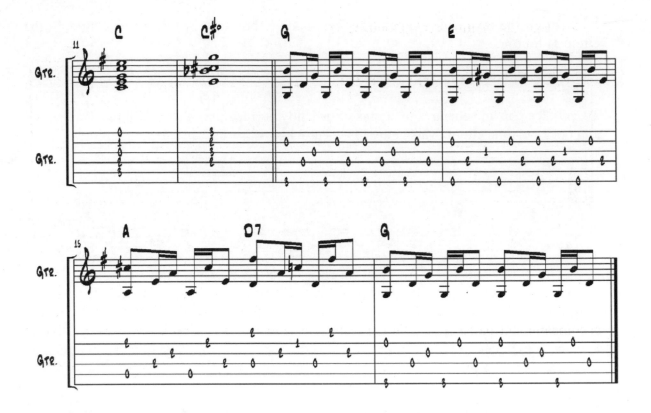

Pentatonic Scale

Here is the A minor pentatonic scale-A, C, D, E and G. This movable pattern begins on the root note. Be sure to play the pattern in all 12 keys.

Ex. 7.23

Ex. 7.24: C minor pentatonic scale

The pentatonic scale is used heavily in rock and blues. In those idioms you can use it to improvise without changing the scale, although you can change scales, if you wish. Refer to one of the video examples of the 12 bar, and improvise along with the chord progression. For a more personalized option, record yourself playing one of the accompaniment patterns so you can cater the length of the song to your liking.. Note: Several companies such as Jamey Aebersold or Alfred publish play-along recordings. The latter includes play- along recordings specifically designed for the guitar.

Hammer ons and Pull offs

Now try embellishing a few notes with some hammer ons and pull-offs. Playing a hammer from a fretted note is the same as hammering from an open string. Just make sure your first finger or the finger you are hammering from keeps pushing down until you proceed to the next note. Otherwise the sound quality will be affected.

Ex. 7.25

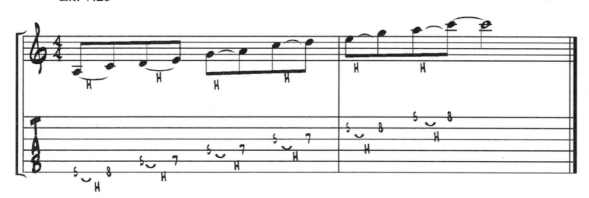

Mastering a pull-off is a bit more difficult than the hammer-on. Before you play a pull off, you have to fret both the note you are pulling off from as the well as the note you are pulling off to. In the example, your fourth finger will be fretting the 8th fret and your first finger will be fretting the 5th fret. Now play the first string. With your fourth finger lightly pluck the first string so that only your first finger is down.

If you did not achieve a sound, don't worry. It will take some practice to master the coordination.

Ex. 7.26

Slides

The slide is achieved by playing a note, and depressing it down while sliding fretwise either higher or lower.

Ex. **7.27**

The bend requires physically bending the string. Start by playing the 7th fret of the 3rd string with your third finger. This enables your 1st and 2nd fingers to help push the string. Now, while keeping the string in contact with the fret, push it up so that it sounds a half step higher.

Ex. 7.28

Once you feel comfortable, push the string it up so that it sounds a whole step higher.

Ex. 7.29

You can also treat the bend as a grace note so that the first note briefly sounds.

Ex. 7.30

Now try bending up and releasing the bend. This is accomplished by keeping the string in contact with the fret both as you bend and straighten the string.

Ex. 7.31

You can also pre-bend the note so that you just hear the release.

Ex. 7.32

Practice all of the above exercises with the DVD and incorporate these licks into your improvisations.

Chapter VIII

Music Therapy Techniques

The Modes

This chapter will help you work though different modes and the typical chord progressions that imply the mode. Modes can be very useful in improvisational sessions with clients. They can help support and challenge what is created during the therapy session. Although we will begin the chapter by reviewing all the modes of the C major scale, all of the exercises will be voiced in G for ease of playing them on guitar. Modes can be broken up into parallel and relative. Parallel means that the mode starts on the same note each time. For the relative mode, the beginning note changes. Notice the notes in any given mode share the same stepwise relationship as its parallel.

Modes of C Major

	Relative	Parallel
Ionian	C D E F G A B C	C D E F G A B C
Dorian	D E F G A B C D	C D Eb F G A Bb C
Phrygian	E F G A B C D E	C Db Eb F G Ab Bb C
Lydian	F G A B C D E F	C D E F# G A B C
Mixolydian	G A B C D E F G	C D E F G A Bb C
Aeolian	A B C D E F G A	C D Eb F G Ab Bb C
Locrian	B C D E F G A B	C Db Eb F Gb Ab Bb C

Notice that Ionian is the same as Major and that Aeolian is the same as natural minor. Also note that the harmonic minor and melodic minor both have modes of their own; however, they are typically used in advanced jazz improvisation and would require in depth study that is beyond the scope of this book.

Compare order of the modes in the key of C with the mode of the G major scale listed below:

G Ionian
A Dorian
B Phrygian
C Lydian
D Mixolydian
E Aeolian
F# Locrian

Here are the notes of G major scale in open position.

Fig. 1

These notes will work for all of the modes of G major, you just need to emphasize certain notes over others. To expand your range on the guitar, the modes will also be presented in moveable two octave patterns starting on the root of each mode. In other words, once you learn the Ionian pattern you can move the pattern so that the fret where your first finger begins, will determine the Ionian mode. For example, if your first finger begins on the third fret, you would play a G Ionian scale. If the first finger begins on the fourth fret, it is an Ab Ionian scale. The same rule would apply for the other patterns and scales.

G Ionian

Fig. 2: Three note per string scale.

As mentioned previously, the G Ionian scale is the same as the major scale. The harmonies that would imply Ionian are the basic I, IV, V. Practice the chord progressions in the example below. Record them using your preferred rhythm and then improvise over the top by using the G Ionian scale.

Fig. 3: Chords in G Ionian

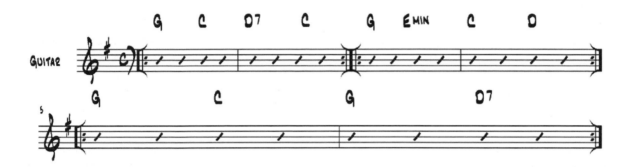

A Dorian

Fig. 4: Three note per string scale

103

The key harmonic sounds of a Dorian scale are the minor i to the minor ii. To achieve this movement in A Dorian, play an A minor chord and slide it up two frets. Move back and forth between the two frets. This movement can be found in Van Morrison's *Moondance*. Another common chord of the Dorian scale would be the major IV. Move between the i to the IV. Incorporate a Latin rhythm and you may hear Santana's *Oye...como va*. You can also combine Dorian mode with the minor scale and switch between the major and minor IV. Many popular rock tunes do this. Try to guess the tune of the chord progression listed below. As with all of the mode exercises, record yourself playing the progression and then improvise along with the recording.

Note: As you improvise in Dorian, you will notice that every note sounds "right." That is because each note is either a chord or a whole step above a tonic chord tone. Consequently, no tone sounds dissonant. For this reason the Dorian mode is extremely accessible in terms of improvising with clients.

Fig. 5: Chords in A Dorian

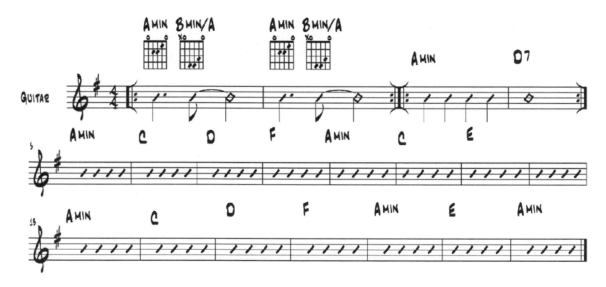

B and E Phrygian

Both scales are presented here. The B Phrygian scale is presented to maintain consistency with the other modes of G major; however, if you are a beginning/intermediate guitar player, start with E Phrygian. Not only is it easy to play but the majority of Phrygian tunes are in E. The common chord progression for Phrygian is the i to bII to bIII. It suggests a Spanish feel. In fact, it is the basis for a Soleares, a common song form in Flamenco music. In the Soleares, the minor i is often used interchangeably with the major I. Consequently, you can use both G and G# if you are in E Phrygian and D and D# if you are playing B Phrygian. The two most common chord progressions are given below.

104

Fig. 6: B Phrygian three note per string scale

Fig. 7: Chords in B Phrygian

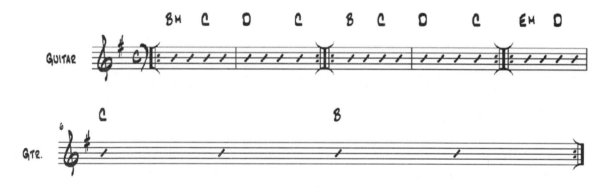

105

Fig.8: E Phrygian scale

Fig. 9: Chords in E Phrygian

C Lydian

This is the other mode that does not have a "wrong" note. Every note is a whole step above the tonic chord. Play through it. It sounds pretty open and seems to suggest movement, as if it is going somewhere. For this reason, the Lydian mode is often featured in movies, particularly children's films, to indicate that the character is pondering something. The common Lydian sound would be the I to II. Both are major. This is what creates the open sound.

Fig. 10: C Lydian scale

Fig.11: C Lydian chords

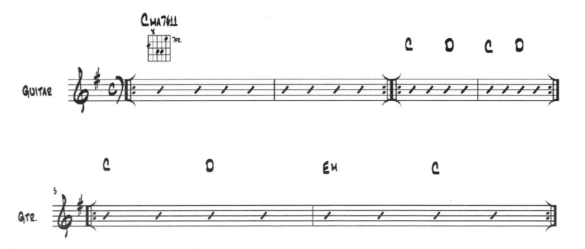

D Mixolydian

The Mixolydian scale can be heard in much of '80's rock. Van Halen's "Jump," Eric Clapton's "Cocaine," and Tina Turner's "The Best" are all songs based on the Mixolydian scale. The b7 is really the key here. The I and bVII are the key harmonic sounds. Mixolydian can be also heard in blues improvisation; however, it is a little trickier than using a pentatonic scale, as you have to change Mixolydian scales with each chord change.

Fig. 12: D Mixolydian scale

Fig. 13: D Mixolydian chords. This exercise uses tablature notation as well.

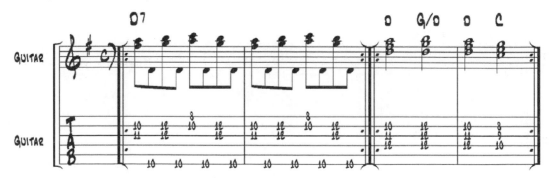

108

E Aeolian

This mode is the same as the natural minor scale. As with the Phrygian and Dorian modes, you can borrow tones from other scales (e.g., Harmonic minor, melodic minor etc). If you are to stay in the Aeolian mode though, remember to maintain the harmonic structure of bVII and a bVI.

Fig. 14: E Aeolian Scale. This scale can start on 12th fret or the open E string.

OR

Fig. 15: E Aeolian Chords

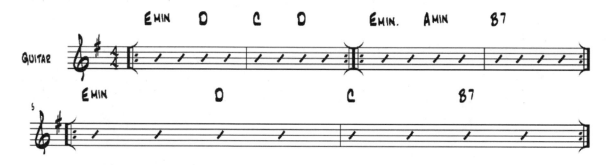

F# Locrian

Begin practicing this mode by trying to sing the tonic. Play around with it for a while, then go back and sing the tonic again. It is very difficult. Many people want to sing G instead of F#. You can hear how this mode would be good for maintaining a feeling of tension. No chord progression will be given for this mode. Just practice improvising over the two chords given below.

Fig. 16: F# Locrian Scale

Fig. 17: F# Locrian chords

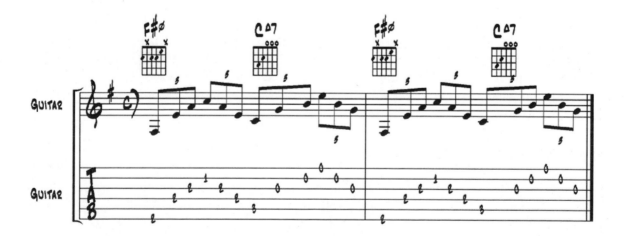

Rules for Improvisation

Rule #1: Loudness Level

Let the soloist lead you whether it is in a clinical or another musical situation. If you are playing louder than the soloist you are too loud, unless of course you have an intentional clinical reason for doing so. Otherwise back off and be supportive. Being softer also helps your ability to listen to what your client is doing and therefore increases your ability to respond.

Rule #2: Question and Answer

Say you were to ask me "How are you doing?" and I were to respond "Tacos." You would either think I misheard you or did not hear you at all. While "tacos" is a legitimate response for a bunch of questions, such as "What did you have for lunch?," "What is your favorite food?" etc., it was not the answer to your question. So what does that mean musically? Well if you or your client play a phrase as a question, think of a phrase that would answer it. Both the antecedent and consequent phrase may be only a few notes long but have them share enough similarities so that they sound cohesive.

Rule #3: Leave Space

Berklee College of Music professor Mick Goodrick once said, "Consider music a creative way to get from one silence to the next." It is in the silence that creativity and musicality can happen. If when you improvise you fill in all the space, where does that leave your client? Let people look forward to the next note you are going to play.

Rule #4: Don't Forget About Dynamics and Tone

Using both these techniques can add variety to an improvisation. Think about some of your favorite bands. While some may be loud at times, it is the shift from soft to loud that creates the tension. Changing volume is done by simply playing louder or softer. Changing the tone can be done by picking closer or farther away from the bridge, changing how the pick strikes the string or even changing from pick to fingers. Experiment!

Open Tunings and Slide Guitar

Some of your clients may have difficulty in playing the guitar in the traditional way. Fortunately, there are several open tunings and a couple of different ways you can play the guitar that allow an inexperienced guitar player to achieve success in playing.

Let's begin with the open tunings. The guitar is tuned E, B, G, D, A, E from high to low (in pitch). However, one can tune the guitar to an open chord such as D or G. An open chord allows someone to play a chord without having to press down on any of the frets.

To tune the guitar to an open D tuning, tune your E strings down a whole step to D, your B string down a whole step to A and your G string down a ½ step to F#. Once all of the strings have been tuned, strum across all of the strings and you should hear a D chord. To play a D# chord simply barre the first fret. To play an E chord barre the second fret and so on. You will notice that your fifth fret has a dot as well as your seventh fret. This is particularly helpful in open D tuning because the dots are your IV and V chords, respectively. Try playing any one of the previously mentioned chord progressions in the open D tuning setting. If you are interested in trying other chord shapes, they are included below.

Fig. 18: Open D Chords

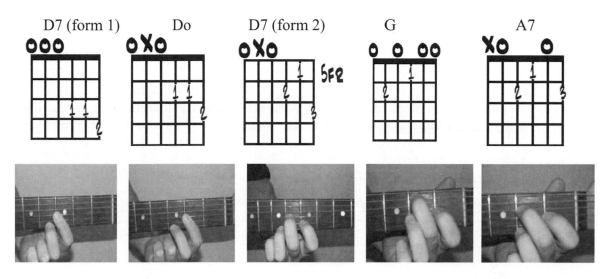

At this point you may be wondering how to utilize this open tuning information when working with a client who does not have the hand strength to barre a fret on the guitar. This is where the use of a guitar slide can be particularly helpful. Slide guitar can be played one of two ways. The first method is achieved by playing the guitar held upright normally. The other is to lay the guitar lying on your lap with the strings facing up. The latter method can be useful for clients with extremely limited motor abilities.

To play slide with the guitar held in the standard manner you must first obtain a slide. A slide can be made from any number of materials e.g., a bottleneck, a wrench socket etc. The only requirement for the slide is that it is hard. You can also find for purchase a plethora of slides at your neighborhood guitar store. Once you have a slide, pick a finger on which to put it. Any finger will work except for the first finger. We recommend the pinky, but some professional musicians like Bonnie Raitt use their middle finger. Take the slide and place it on the strings at the fifth fret making sure it is directly above the metal fret wire (otherwise it will sound out of tune). Do not press down. Now strum. You should hear a G chord. Try it on the 7th fret for A and the 12th fret for D. For the stylistic sliding sound, keep the slide on the strings as you are changing chords. You may notice extra notes sounding from behind the slide. These can be eliminated by gently placing

113

your fingers on the strings to mute them. Everything in front of the slide should sound and every thing behind it should not.

In order to play the guitar on your lap, lay the guitar flat on its back with the strings facing up. Hold the slide inside a slight fist. Then follow the rules described previously.

After some experimentation let's try playing in D open tuning in a 12 bar progression. Here is an example of some riffs in the style of Elmore James.

     Ex. 8.01: D tuning. View DVD.

     Ex. 8.02:

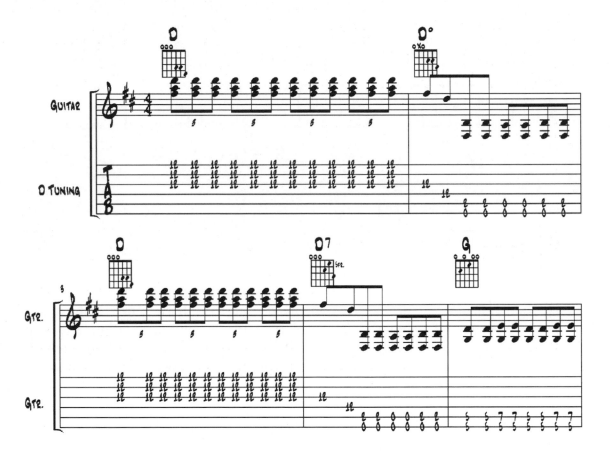

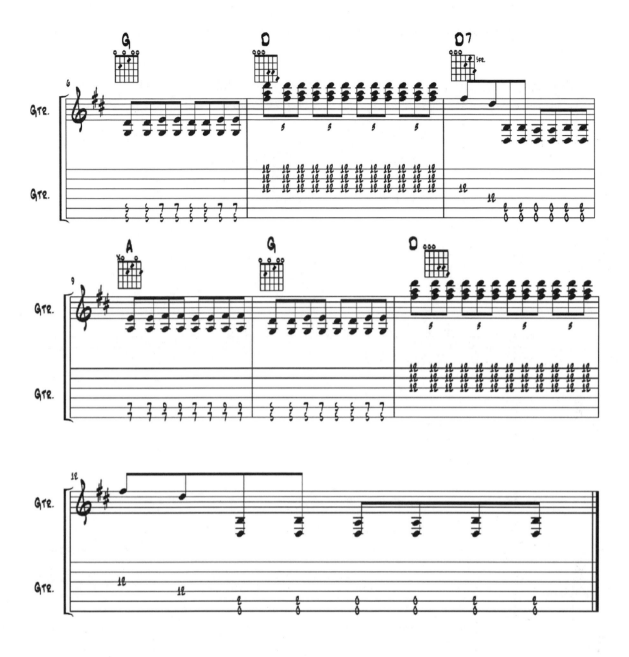

Open G

You can also try these techniques in an open G tuning. For open G, tune both E strings down to D and the A string down to G. As you experiment with the chords you may notice that they sound similar to Keith Richards' style, who was influenced by Muddy Waters. Consequently, there are some Muddy Waters riffs to try in the next exercise. As with open D tuning, the I chord is played by strumming the open strings, the IV chord is played by barring across the fifth fret and your V is found by barring across the seventh fret. Additional options include open position chords.

Fig. 19: Open G chords

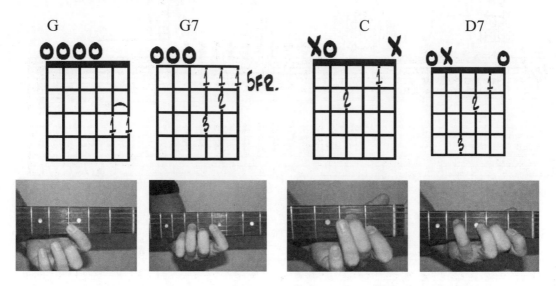

Ex. 8.03: G tuning. View DVD.

Ex. 8.04: Riffs in the style of Muddy Waters

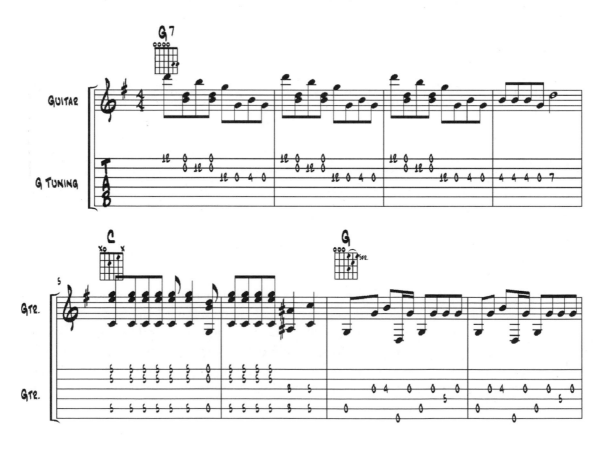

116

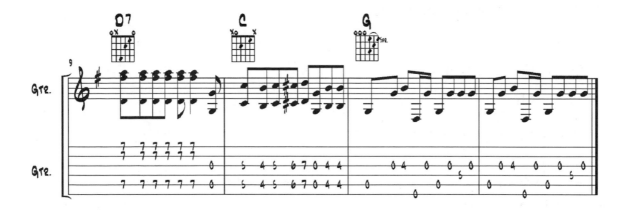

Two Handed Techniques

This next example can be heard in the stylings of Michael Hedges, Billy McLaughlin, Preston Reed, and Kaki King to name a few. All the notes are produced by hammering on. You will not need a pick. We have chosen to present this excerpt in DADGAD tuning. This particular tuning is appealing, as it can sound either major, minor, or both. For the bass/accompaniment component, take the index finger of your right hand and strike the 4th, 5th and 6th strings at the fifth fret. (This gives you a nice power chord). Now do this on the 3rd fret, then the first fret and then pull off so the open strings sound.

Ex. 8.05:

For simplicity this exercise is presented using only tablature notation.

For the melody, use your left hand to hammer the first notes on each string and pull off the others. Again the only hand that should be moving is your left.

Ex. 8.06:

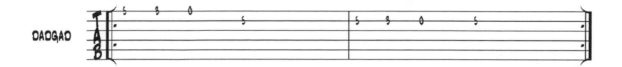

117

The last example combines both parts.

Ex. 8.07

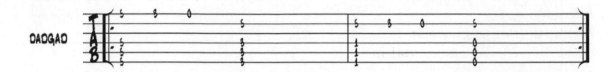

 Make sure to allow yourself time to learn this material. You don't have to play it exactly as written. Experiment and have fun.

Chapter IX

Jazz Guitar

Introduction to Chords

The main difference between the previous material we have covered and the material in this chapter is the harmonic structure. Up to this point, we have been working mainly with three part harmony. Jazz usually has four or more part harmony. The most common four part chords were presented at the end of chapter V. In this chapter, we will be exploring some more harmonic options.

Let's begin by fingering the E shape dom. 7 and minor 7's as suggested below.

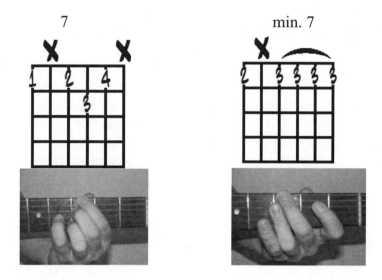

By eliminating the 5th immediately above the root, the chords will sound less muddy.

Here are a few more common jazz chords. These are the 6 chords. The major 6 chords can be used in place of Maj. 7 and Dom. 7 because they are major and do not have a 7. Try using them in any song to replace the maj. 7 or 7. Note: The root note for these chords is the lowest note.

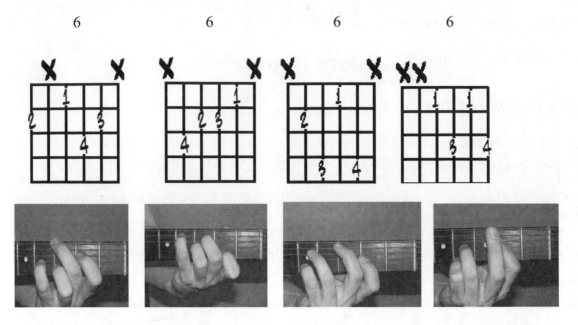

To learn these chords, we will break down the process just as we did with the open chords. Begin by practicing some of the most accessible chords such as the change from the sixth string root, E shape, Bb Maj. 7 chord to the Bb 6 chord. If you need extra time to switch, add a rest or two. Once you are comfortable moving between the chords, practice moving through the circle of 4ths. Next, try the same thing with chords that have the root note on the fifth or fourth string. Then try a combination of chords that have root notes on different strings.

Fig. 1

Once you are comfortable with the first exercise add the dominant 7 chord. Note: In addition to maj. 7, a major 7 chord can be indicated by any of these symbols- M7, Δ or Δ7.

Fig. 2

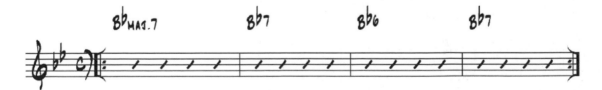

Now let's try to move between the minor chords, switching from a min. 7 to a minor 6. Note that A minor 6 chord can be substituted for a min. 7 chord.

    Min. 6   Min. 6   Min. 6   Min. 6

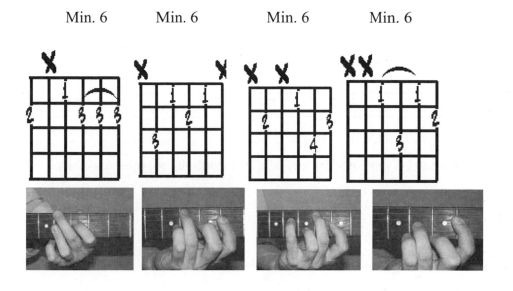

Fig. 3

As with the previous exercises, start out with the chords that have a root note on the 6th string and then move on to the chords that have the root note on the 5th and 4th strings. Try substituting a min. 6 for min. 7 or a minor chord in some of your favorite songs. Another common chord is the min.(maj. 7). It is a minor triad with a major 7 on top.

Min. (maj. 7)   Min. (maj. 7)   Min. (maj. 7)

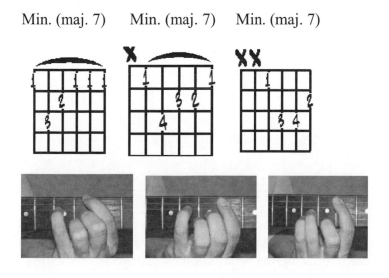

The min.(maj 7) is commonly used as a passing chord between a minor triad and a minor 7.

Fig. 4

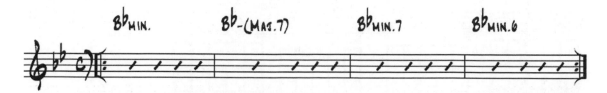

Note that a minor chord can be indicated by any of these symbols: m, min., or −.

Another chord that can add color to your playing is the Augmented chord. Augmented chords can be indicated by these symbols: A, + or aug.

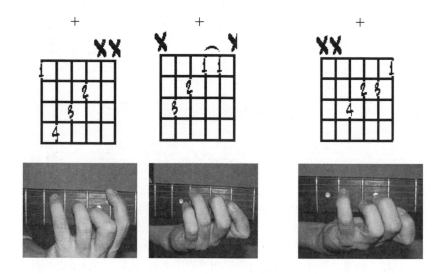

Here is a common chord progression that uses an augmented chord. This progression is a nice way to move from a I chord to a IV. Although this progression is found most often in jazz music, it can be applied to other styles, as well.

Fig. 5

Once you are comfortable with all of the above exercises. Try playing through them again using the staccato strumming technique. Then apply the technique to the chord changes for "I've Got Rhythm". These chords are the foundation for many jazz standards.

Ex. 9.01

Chord Substitutions

Now that you are playing jazz chords, let's try some chord substitutions. Jazz music, at its foundation, prominently consists of three types of chords: ii=min. 7 or min. 7 b5, V= dom. 7 and I= maj. 7. The I chord is your home base, the V chord resolves to the I and the ii leads to the V.

As always, there are exceptions. The most notable would be the diminished chord. The diminished chord wants to resolve a half step higher than its root note and it can resolve to any type of chord.

Now that you understand the basic jazz chords, let's look at some new concepts. The chords listed are more commonly used and are intended as a starting point. You can easily spend the rest of your life creating new and different chord voicings.

Concept 1: ii chord

A min. 7= min. 9, min. 6, min. 11, min. 13 and in some case min./maj. 7 or min. 7 b5.

Note: In all the chords listed the root note is the lowest note of the chord unless it is labeled with an open circle. The open circle means the root is not being played but indicates where you would find the root note. A note labeled with a "T" indicates that you play the note with the thumb on the left hand. This is done by wrapping your thumb around the top and fretting a note. You are not meant to play on the fingertip of the thumb, as this would prove almost impossible. You just need to have a portion of the thumb pressing the string into the fret. If you have small hands and are unable to do this technique, do not worry about it. Simply play the remaining notes and leave off the root.

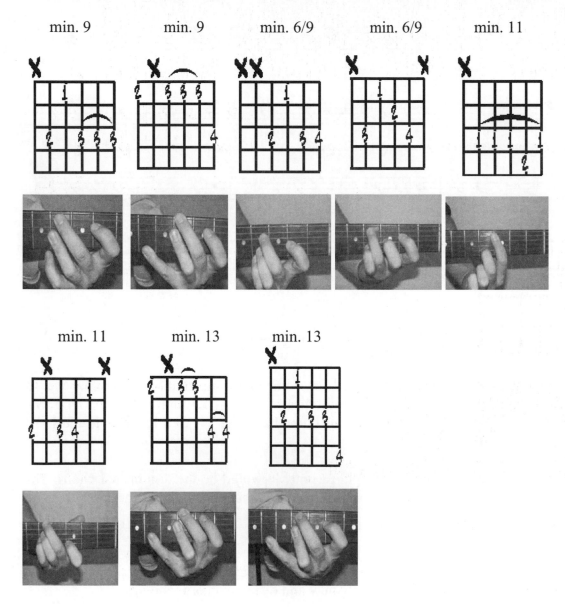

V chords : A Dom. 7= 9, 13, #9, b9, #11 etc.

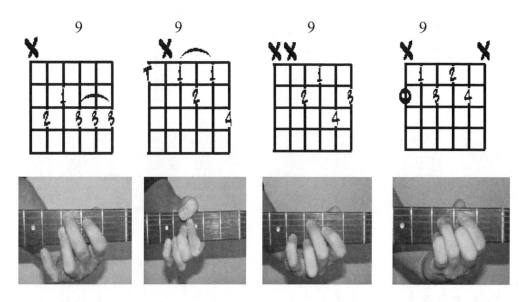

Note: The 6/9 chords can be used as substitutions for both maj. 7 and 7 chords.

6/9   6/9

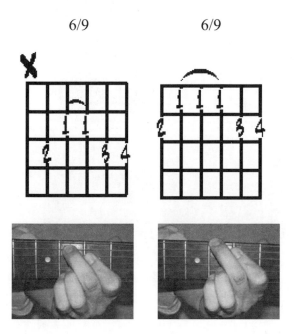

Note: The 11th in these chords is sharped so that it will not clash with the third of the chord.

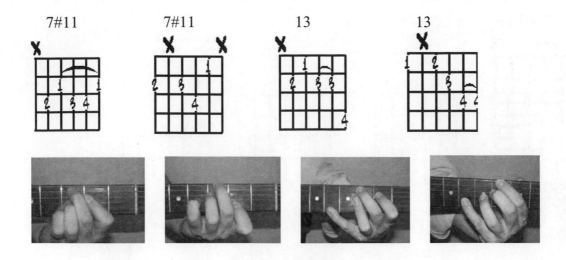

Note: Since V chords generally serve to move towards a resolution, you can even increase their dissonance by flatting or sharping the 9, flatting the 5 (#11) or flatting the 13 (+7). These chords will be labeled as 7 alt.

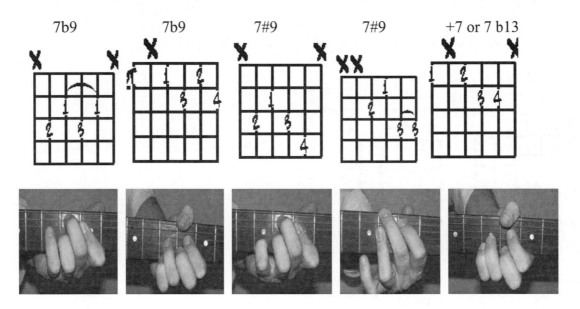

+7 or b13

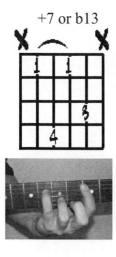

I chords:

Maj. 7= Maj. 9, 6/9, Maj. 13, Maj. 7 add 6 and in some cases Maj. 7 #11.

Maj. 9   Maj. 9

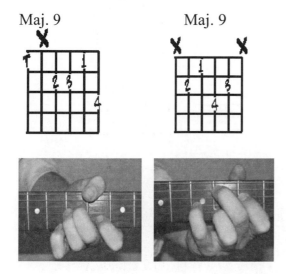

Note: The 11 in these chords is sharped so that it will not clash with the third of the chord.

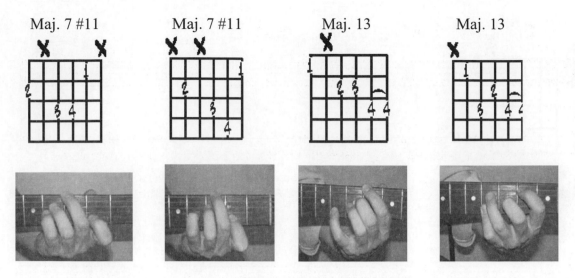

Maj. 7 #11   Maj. 7 #11   Maj. 13   Maj. 13

Note: Because a minor 7 can become minor 9 or 11 and a major 7 can become a maj. 9, a 9, or a 13, then reverse is also true. A 13 can be simplified into just a major triad. The minor 9's can be simplified into a minor triad etc. So if you see a chord symbol that you are not yet able to play, simply reduce it to a triad and it will serve the same function.

Concept 2: A ii chord can be placed in front of a V chord: /V /I / = /ii V /I /

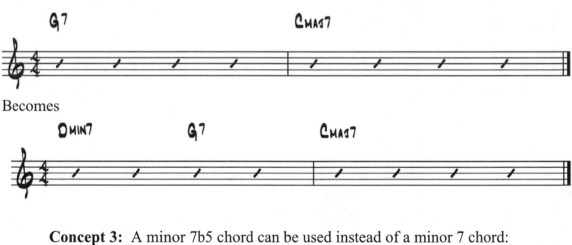

Becomes

Concept 3: A minor 7b5 chord can be used instead of a minor 7 chord:
/ii min. 7 V7 /I maj. 7 / = /ii min. 7 b5 V7 /I maj. 7   /

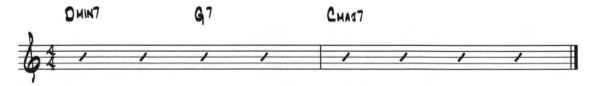

Becomes

Concept 4: If you have a minor chord that lasts two measures this may become boring for a listener to hear. Try playing this progression to add movement.

/ ii min. 7   /ii min. 7   /= /ii   ii min. (maj. 7)   / ii min. 7   ii min. 6   /

Becomes

Concept 5: Just as you can add a ii min. 7 chord in front of any V7, you can add a V7 chord in front of any other chord. You can combine this concept with the second concept by adding the ii min. 7 as well.

/V7   /I maj. 7   / = /II7 V7/I maj. 7   / or /G7   /C maj. 7/ = /D7 G7/C maj. 7 /

Becomes

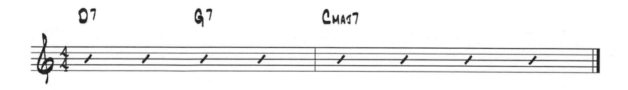

Concept 6: The most tension filled interval in a dominant 7 chord is the tri-tone, the interval between the 3rd and the 7th. This interval is shared between two dominant 7 chords. For example, in looking at the G7 and Db7 chords, the tri-tones are B and F, and F and Cb receptively. Because both chords share such a tension filled interval, they can be used interchangeably. This substitution is known as a tri-tone substitution.

/V7   /I maj. 7   / = /bII7   /I maj. 7   / or /G7   /Cmaj. 7/ = /Db7 /C maj. 7   /

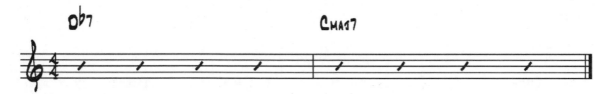

Is the same as

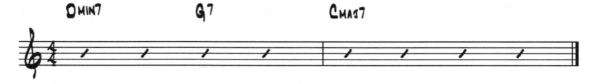

Concept 7: This combines concepts 3, 5 and 6.

/D min. 7   G7   /C maj. 7   / = /C# min. 7 F#7 C min. 7 F7   /Bb maj. 7   /

Can become

130

Concept 8: Diminished chords are built by stacking minor 3rds. Therefore a C dim. contains the same notes as the Eb dim. , F# dim and A dim. chords. Since a dom. 7 b9 contains a diminished chord [G 7b9= G (B D F Ab)] they also can be substituted a minor 3rd apart.

/G7   /C maj. 7   / = /G7   Bb7   Db7   E7 /C maj. 7   /

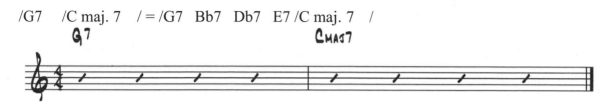

Can be any of the following

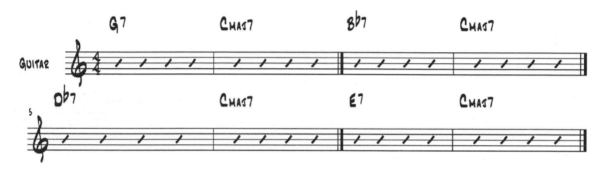

Jazz improvisation

The key difference between improvising the way Chapter VII and VIII demonstrated and jazz improvisation is that in jazz you have to be able to play the chord changes, both harmonically and melodically. The following exercises will lay the foundations for this. Please note that this may take years to master. Let's start with a blues progression. Below is a 12-bar with jazz harmonies.

Fig. 5

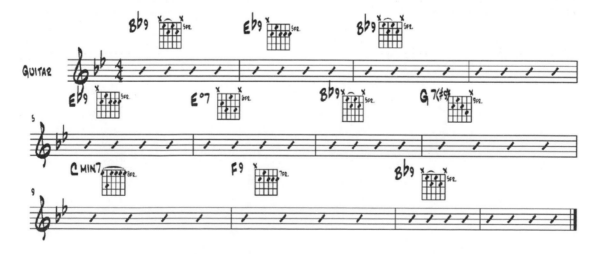

131

However, for simplicity and easier improvisation, it can be reduced to this.

Fig.6

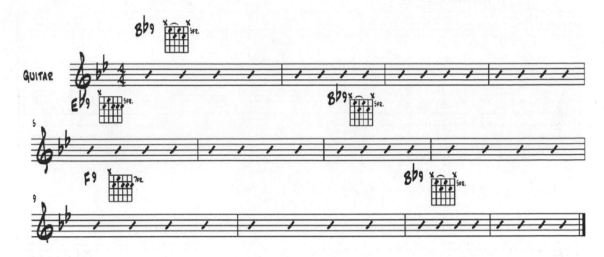

First we will start with playing the changes melodically. The easiest way to do this is through arpeggios. Since they are comprised of chord tones you know that all the notes will sound "right."

Fig. 7: Bb7 Arpeggio

Fig. 8: Eb7 Arpeggio

Fig. 9: F7 Arpeggio

The 3rd of the chord is the note that implies the chord change. Try shifting rhythm so that 3rd is on the strong beats, either 1 or 3.

Fig. 10: Bb

Fig. 11: Eb

Fig. 12: F

Now let's incorporate the arpeggios into a blues progression.

Fig. 13

So that it does not sound like you are playing only arpeggios, you can add notes from the Mixolydian scales. Play Bb Mixolyian over a Bb7 chord, an Eb Mixolydian over the Eb7 chord and a F Mixolydian scale over the F7 chord. To fill in the gaps use the corresponding Mixolydian scales.

Fig. 14: Bb Mixolydian

Fig. 15: Eb Mixolydian

Fig. 16: F Mixolydian

Putting it together

The two most important notes in a chord are the 3rd and 7th. To really sound like you are improvising over the changes, you want to play those two notes on the strong beats e.g., 1 and 3. As you learned the 3rd introduces the chord. Conversely the 7th sounds like it wants to leave the chord. In other words, when you begin a phrase you want the first part to emphasize the 3rd and as you are preparing to change chords you want to emphasize the 7th. You could manage to improvise by just playing those two notes. However, add the arpeggio and Mixolydian scales to create a more full sound. Note: Avoid playing the 4th note of the mixolydian scales as it clashes with the 3rd of the chord. It still works as a passing note, however.

Putting it together blues:

Fig. 17

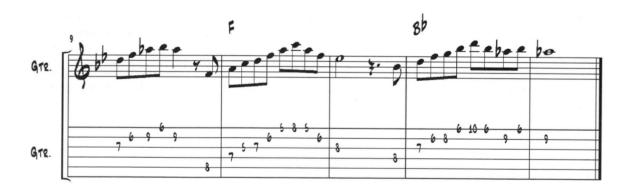

137

Chapter X

Funk Guitar

Introduction to Funk Guitar

To learn to play funk successfully, you must first be able to feel all the 16th notes in a beat. This is achieved by practicing the following exercise. Start with an E9 chord (the funkiest of all funk chords). Finger it, then play it as a percussive chuck on for several measures of 16th notes. Remember to count 1 ee & ah, 2 ee & ah etc. You will strum down on the beat, up on the "ee," down on "&" and up on the "ah." (Make sure to use a metronome while practicing this exercise). Once this feels comfortable, press down on the first beat. Next, play the "&", then add the "ee," and lastly the "ah." Adding the last two values are more difficult to master because they occur on upstrokes and also because it is difficult to resist the natural urge to play rhythmic chucks on the off beat. Once you have managed to isolate each fraction of the beat, try doing two chords per beat, then three and then four. All the variations are listed below. Start with the first and once you are comfortable, move on to the next example.

Ex. 10.01

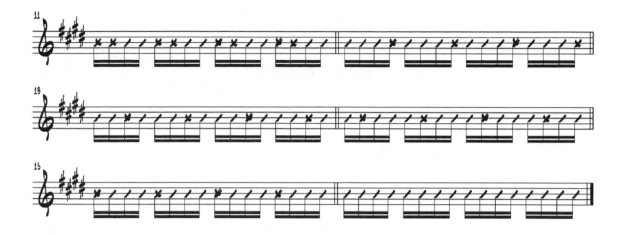

Next, let's add some variety to each measure. Try the next exercise with a familiar I, IV, V progression.

Fig. 1

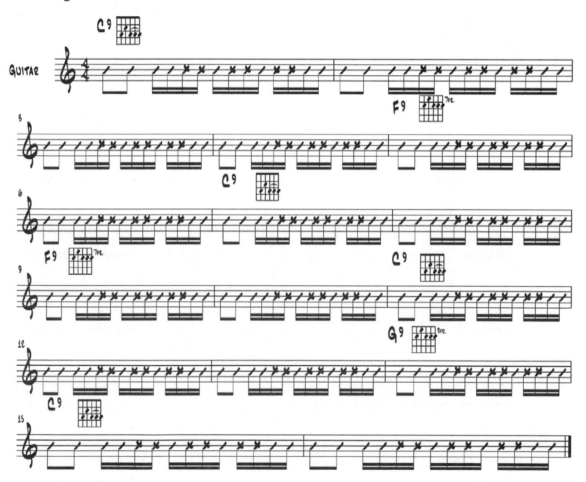

Bossa Nova

The Bossa Nova groove comes from a Brazilian style of guitar playing. It was popularized by artists such as Antonio Carlos Jobim. Almost everything that has been introduced in this book emphasizes beats 2 and 4. However the Bossa Nova emphasizes beats 1 and 3. Start by taking a chord such as C maj. 9 and playing a bass note on beats 1 and 3.

Ex. 10.02

Now comes the difficult part, playing the syncopation of the chords.

Ex. 10.03

It actually seems easier to combine the two parts. Instead of isolating the chord part after you have learned the bass, play them together. Again, give this time. Now try it with any of your favorite songs. It does not matter if it is not Latin.

Ex. 10.04

R & B styles

This style of playing was popularized by Curtis Mayfield and Jimi Hendrix. Instead of playing a chord by simply strumming, you can add embellishments. These are the same embellishments that you learned at the beginning of this book, but now are accompanying barre chords. Familiarizing yourself with the C and G barre shapes will be useful for these exercises. Try these licks.

Ex. 10.05

The same lick can be used to imply a major or minor chord.

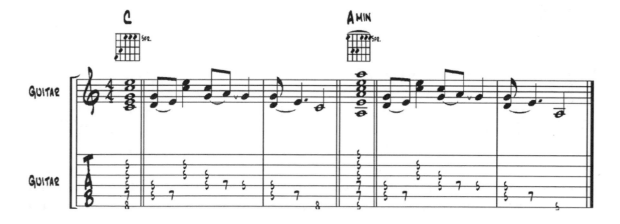

Ex. 10.06

Ex. 10.07

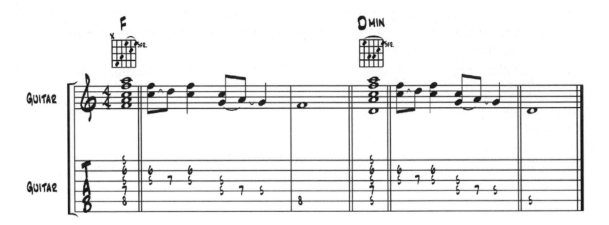

Now try incorporating the riffs you have just learned into your favorite song.

142

Chapter XI

Guitar Maintenance

Guitar Humidifiers

There are many different types of guitar humidifiers on the market. We suggest that you purchase one for your acoustic guitar and check it regularly. Electric guitars may not require one. Ask your retailer for recommendations.

Changing Strings

- Remove the string from the guitar.
- After running a string through the peg, push peg down into hole.
  - Run string upwards through tuning peg hole with hole positioned parallel with the direction of the string.
- Be sure to leave at least 3 inches of slack in the string before proceeding to next step!
- Pull end of string *under* itself, toward the outside of the neck.
- Pull string tight and fast!
- Pull the string back towards the center *over* itself.
- Make a crease in the string at the base of the tuning peg by pushing down.
- Hold the crease down with your finger while turning the tuning peg so that the string winds towards the *center* of the guitar.

Set Up

Just as any car needs an oil change every three thousand miles, your guitar should be set up regularly. What is a set up? It could be called a tune up. The set up means adjusting the truss rod, adjusting the action, and checking it out for any other more serious problems. How often do you need one? It varies from place to place, depending on climate and humidity. While you may need your guitar set up more often, at a minimum, it should be set up every six months. Where does one get a guitar set up? Most guitar stores offer this service. However, use caution when selecting a repair shop. Ask around, ask other guitar players, especially seasoned players. While a set up is a good thing, if it is done incorrectly, it can cause damage to the guitar.

Guitar Skills for Music Therapists and Music Educators
DVD Track List
Total Run Time: 1 hr 35 min 35 sec (01:35:35)

Title: (Length - Min/Sec - Rounded to the second)
1 - Introduction (01:48)
2 - Chapter I: The Basics (22:05)
3 - Chapter II: I Know C, A, G, E and D... Now What? (14:15)
4 - Chapter III: Fingerpicking (11:13)
5 - Chapter IV: Flatpicking (13:20)
6 - Chapter V: Barre Chords (01:20)
7 - Chapter VI: Power Chords - Are You Ready to Rock? (01:05)
8 - Chapter VII: The Blues (12:40)
9 - Chapter VIII: Music Therapy Techniques (05:18)
10 - Chapter IX: Jazz Guitar (01:55)
11 - Chapter X: Other Styles (08:37)
12 - Chapter XI: Guitar Maintenance (01:59)

Title 1 - Introduction (Time: 01:48)
> 1 – Introduction
> 2 – Holding the Guitar
> 3 – Standard Tuning

Title 2 - Chapter I: The Basics   (Time: 22:05)
> 1 – Exercise 1.01 – G to Em
> 2 – Exercise 1.02 – Em to C
> 3 – Exercise 1.03 – C to D7
> 4 – Exercise 1.04 – D7 to G
> 5 – Exercise 1.05 – D7 to G: Strum for 4 Beats & Rest for 4 Beats
> 6 – Exercise 1.06 – D7 to G: Strum for 4 Beats & Rest for 2 Beats
> 7 – Exercise 1.07 – D7 to G: Strum for 3 Beats & Rest for 1 Beats
> 8 – Exercise 1.08 – D7 to G: Strum Without Any Rests
> 9 – Exercise 1.09 – G - Em - C - D7
> 10 – Exercise 1.10 – '50's Rock Chord Progression
> 11 – Exercise 1.11 – D to Bm
> 12 – Exercise 1.12 – Bm to G
> 13 – Exercise 1.13 – G to A7
> 14 – Exercise 1.14 – A7 to D
> 15 – Exercise 1.15 – D - Bm - G - A7
> 16 – Exercise 1.16 – Down in the Valley
> 17 – Exercise 1.17 – C to Am
> 18 – Exercise 1.18 – Am to F
> 19 – Exercise 1.19 – F to G7
> 20 – Exercise 1.20 – G7 to C

Title 8 - Chapter VII: The Blues (Time: 12:40)

    1 – Exercise 7.01 – Open Position Shuffle: C
    2 – Exercise 7.02 – Open Position Shuffle: G
    3 – Exercise 7.03 – Open Position Shuffle: E
    4 – Exercise 7.04 – Open Position Shuffle: A
    5 – Exercise 7.05 – Open Position Shuffle: D
    6 – Exercise 7.06 – Open 12-Bar Blues in A
    7 – Exercise 7.07 – Open 8-Bar Blues in G
    8 – Exercise 7.08 – Moveable Shuffle: Root on the 6th String
    9 – Exercise 7.09 – Moveable Shuffle: Root on the 5th String
    10 – Exercise 7.10 – 12-Bar Blues with Moveable Shuffle Patterns in C
    11 – Exercise 7.11 – Open Boogie Bass in C
    12 – Exercise 7.12 – Open Boogie Bass in A
    13 – Exercise 7.13 – Open Boogie Bass in G
    14 – Exercise 7.14 – Open Boogie Bass in E
    15 – Exercise 7.15 – Open Boogie Bass in D
    16 – Exercise 7.16 – Moveable Boogie in A: Beginning on the 6th String
    17 – Exercise 7.17 – Moveable Boogie in D: Beginning on the 5th String
    18 – Exercise 7.18 – Open 12-Bar Blues with Boogie Bass in G
    19 – Exercise 7.19 – Moveable 12-Bar Blues with Boogie Bass in A
    20 – Exercise7.20 – The Box
    21 – Exercise 7.21 – 12-Bar Box in A
    22 – Exercise 7.22 – "Ice Cream" Changes with the Travis Pick
    23 – Exercise 7.23 – A Minor Pentatonic Scale
    24 – Exercise 7.24 – C Minor Pentatonic Scale
    25 – Exercise 7.25 – A Minor Pentatonic Scale with Hammmer-ons
    26 – Exercise 7.26 – A Minor Pentatonic Scale with Pull-offs
    27 – Exercise 7.27 – Slides
    28 – Exercise 7.28 – Bending Notes Up a Half Step
    29 – Exercise 7.29 – Bending Notes Up a Whole Step
    30 – Exercise 7.30 – Bending as a Grace Note
    31 – Exercise 7.31 – Bending Notes Up & Releasing the Bend
    32 – Exercise 7.32 – Pre-Bending Notes

Title 9 - Chapter VIII: Music Therapy Techniques (Total Time: 05:18)

    1 – Exercise 8.01 – Open D Tuning & Slide Guitar
    2 – Exercise 8.02 – Open D Tuning: 12-Bar Progression in the Style of Elmore James
    3 – Exercise 8.03 – Open G Tuning
    4 – Exercise 8.04 – Open G Tuning: Riffs in the Style of Muddy Waters
    5 – Exercise 8.05 – Two Handed Techniques: Right Hand
    6 – Exercise 8.06 – Two Handed Techniques: Left Hand
    7 – Exercise 8.07 – Two Handed Techniques: Right & Left Hand Combined

Title 10 - Chapter IX: Jazz Guitar (Total Time: 01:55)
    1 – Exercise 9.01 – Rhythm Changes

Title 11 - Chapter X: Other Styles (Total Time: 08:37)
    1 – Exercise 10.01 – Funk Guitar
    2 – Exercise 10.02 – Bossa Nova: Bass on Beats 1 & 3
    3 – Exercise 10.03 – Bossa Nova: Syncopated Chords
    4 – Exercise 10.04 – Bossa Nova: Combining the Bass Notes & Chords
    5 – Exercise 10.05 – R & B Styles: C & Am
    6 – Exercise 10.06 – R & B Styles: C Chord
    7 – Exercise 10.07 – R & B Styles: F & Dm

Title 12 - Chapter XI: Guitar Maintenance (Total Time: 01:59)
    1 – Changing Strings